PAPER CUT
PLANET

Over 150 paper cutting patterns

Kai Iwami

D&C

Artful and inspiring, paper cutting is a celebrated craft practiced around the globe. From Japan to the United States, Sweden to Sri Lanka, paper and scissors are used to decorate, celebrate and commemorate.

Pack your scissors and some colorful paper, then follow the step-by-step guide to learn a few basic folding techniques. You'll be ready to embark on a paper cutting journey in no time! Before you know it, you'll be using the templates to create professional-looking paper cutting designs for all occasions.

Each collection of motifs includes fun and easy project ideas for using the templates, such as scrapbooks, greeting cards, stationery and gift wrap...the possibilities are endless!

Welcome to the wonderful world of paper cutting! I hope you enjoy your stay!

—Kai Iwami

CONTENTS

BEFORE YOU BEGIN

THE PROJECTS

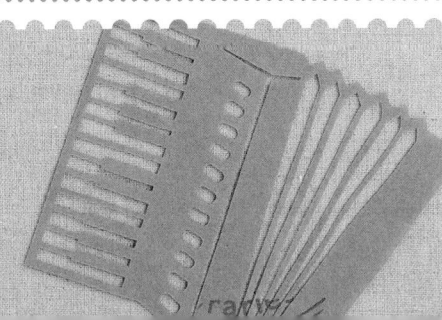

TOOLS AND MATERIALS

You won't need any specialized tools or hard-to-find materials to get started on the projects in this book. In fact, you may have everything you need at home already.

Tools

Pencil: Use a mechanical pencil to copy the template onto tracing paper.

Pen: Use a ballpoint pen to transfer the design from tracing paper to origami paper.

Tracing Paper: Use transparent paper to copy the templates from the book.

Scissors: Use sharp scissors to cut along the outline of the designs. It is important to find a pair that is comfortable and correctly sized, since this will influence the accuracy of your cutting.

Craft Knife: Use a sharp-bladed craft knife to cut the smaller, more detailed areas of the designs. Craft knives offer more precision than scissors.

Cutting Mat: Use a cutting mat to protect your work surface.

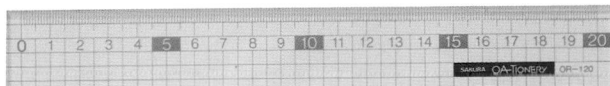

Ruler: Use a ruler when tracing designs with straight lines. Transparent rulers are helpful because they allow you to see your work better.

Tape: Use tape to prevent the tracing paper from moving while copying a design.

Materials

Origami Paper: This brightly colored paper is ideal for paper cutting because it is thin, which allows it to be cut easily, even when folded several times. Origami paper is available in 6" (15 cm) and 3" (7.5 cm) square sheets and is usually colored on one side and white on the other. Origami paper is sold in multi-colored packs at arts and craft stores, office supply stores, and online.

Textured Paper: Add interest to your paper cutting with textured paper, which has a naturally irregular texture and is colored on both sides. A textured Japanese paper called *washi* has been used in origami for over a thousand years. Textured paper can be found in arts and craft stores and online.

Patterned Paper: Add color to your paper cutting with patterned paper, which is available in a wide variety of designs, including polka dots, tie-dye, stripes, and plaid. Patterned paper is sold at arts and crafts stores and online.

Wrapping Paper: Use decorative wrapping paper for large scale designs. Wrapping paper comes in great patterns, so it can even be trimmed down to size for small designs. Wrapping paper can be found at arts and craft stores, discount stores, and online.

FOLDING TECHNIQUES

This book uses two types of folds: geometric folds and accordion folds. The more folds you make, the more images you produce in your finished paper cutting design.

Folding Terms & Symbols

All of the folding techniques in this book involve two simple folds: the valley fold and the mountain fold.

VALLEY FOLD

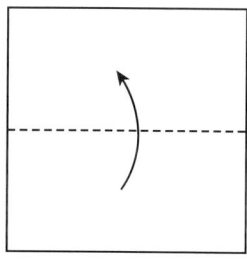

With the right side facing up, fold the paper up, so the crease points down. The symbol for a valley fold is a dashed line.

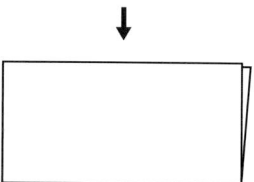

MOUNTAIN FOLD

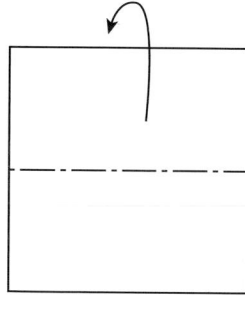

With the right side facing up, fold the paper down, so the crease points up. The symbol for a valley fold is a dashed and dotted line.

Geometric Folds

SINGLE GEOMETRIC FOLD (produces 2 images)

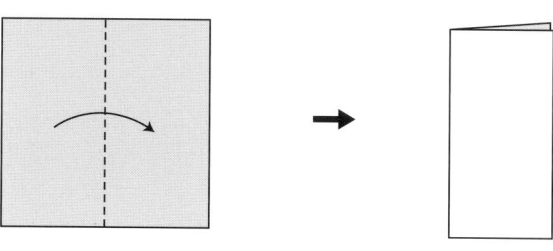

1. With the right side facing up, fold the paper in half vertically to form a rectangle.

Completed view of the single geometric fold.

DOUBLE GEOMETRIC FOLD (produces 4 images)

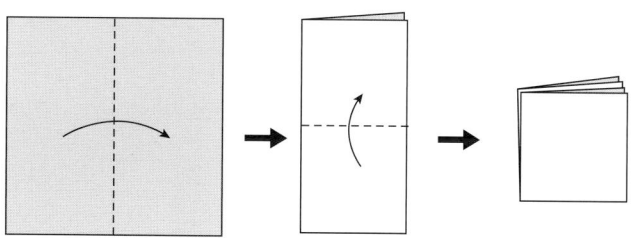

1. With the right side facing up, fold the paper in half vertically to form a rectangle.

2. With the wrong side facing up, fold the rectangle in half horizontally.

Completed view of the double geometric fold.

TRIPLE GEOMETRIC FOLD (produces 6 images)

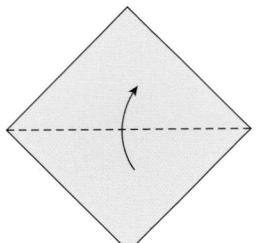 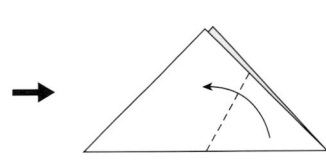 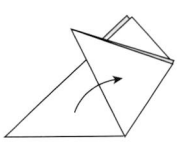 

1. With the right side facing up, fold the paper in half to form a triangle.

2. Fold the right corner of the triangle up at a 60° angle using the template on page 9.

3. Fold the left corner of the triangle up at a 60° angle to meet the crease made in Step #2.

Completed view of the triple geometric fold.

QUADRUPLE GEOMETRIC FOLD (produces 8 images)

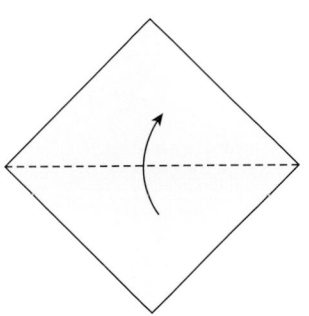 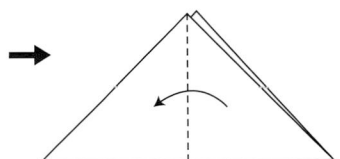 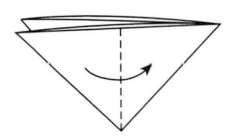 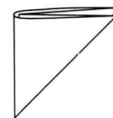

1. With the right side facing up, fold the paper in half to form a triangle.

2. Fold the triangle in half again.

3. Fold the triangle in half once more.

Completed view of the quadruple geometric fold.

SEXTUPLE GEOMETRIC FOLD (produces 12 images)

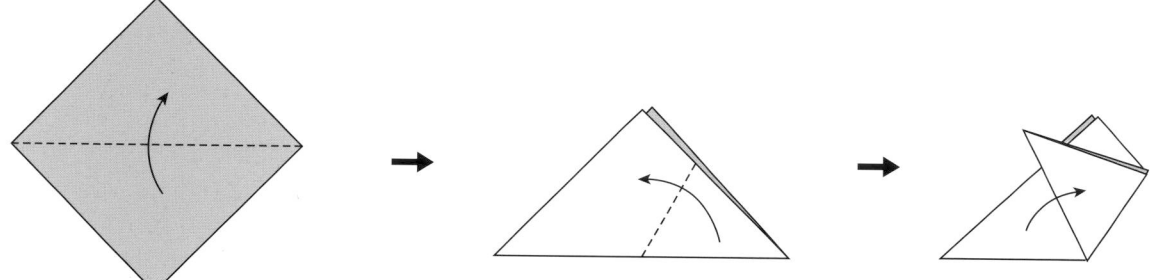

1. With the right side facing up, fold the paper in half to form a triangle.

2. Fold the right corner of the triangle up at a 60° angle using the template on page 9.

3. Fold the left corner of the triangle up at a 60° angle to meet the crease made in Step #2.

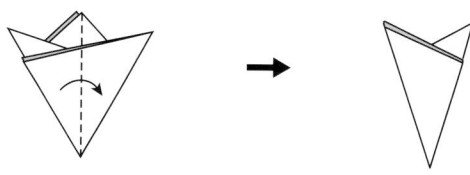

4. Fold the triangle in half vertically.

Completed view of the sextuple geometric fold.

Folding Template

Use this template for the triple geometric fold and the sextuple geometric fold.

Bring right corner of triangle to meet this line.

Fold right corner of triangle along this line.

Fold left corner of triangle to meet dashed line.

Align triangle center here.

60°

Accordion Folds

DOUBLE ACCORDION FOLD (produces 4 images)

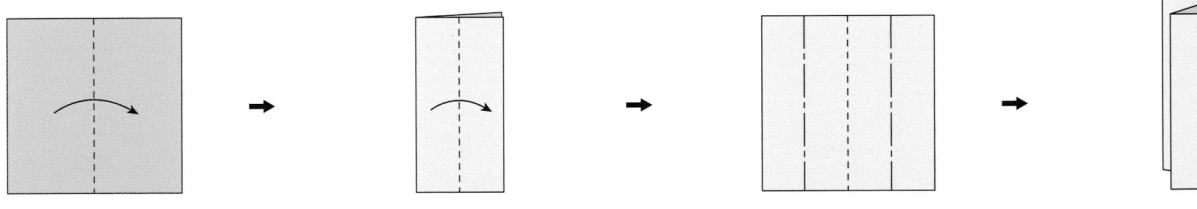

1. With the right side facing up, fold the paper in half vertically to form a rectangle.

2. Fold the rectangle in half again.

3. Unfold the paper. There should be 3 creases.

4. With the wrong side facing up, refold the paper along the creases, alternating between mountain and valley folds.

TRIPLE ACCORDION FOLD (produces 6 images)

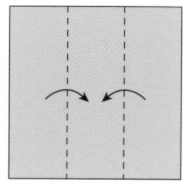

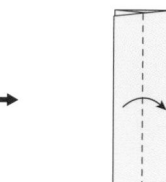

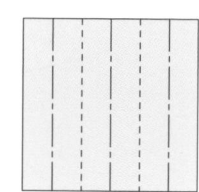

1. With the right side facing up, fold the paper into thirds vertically.

2. Fold the rectangle in half again.

3. Unfold the paper. There should be 5 creases.

4. With the wrong side facing up, refold the paper along the creases, alternating between mountain and valley folds.

QUADRUPLE ACCORDION FOLD (produces 8 images)

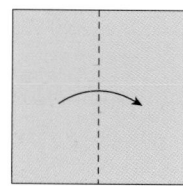

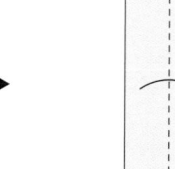

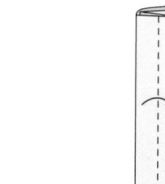

1. With the right side facing up, fold the paper in half vertically to form a rectangle.

2. Fold the rectangle in half again.

3. Fold the rectangle in half once more.

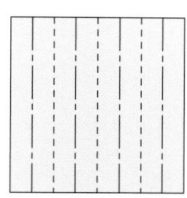

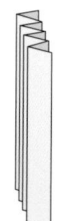

4. Unfold the paper. There should be 7 creases.

5. With the wrong side facing up, refold the paper along the creases, alternating between mountain and valley folds.

PAPER CUTTING TIPS

Here are a few simple tips to keep in mind before you get started. These hints will help you to create beautiful, professional-looking paper cutting designs.

How to Use Scissors

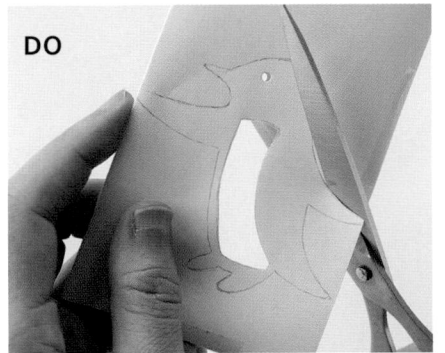

DO

Guide the paper into the blades of the scissors to produce smooth and accurate cuts.

DON'T

Don't use the tips of the scissors because they offer less control and lead to jagged cuts.

How to Use the Craft Knife

Hold the craft knife the same way you would hold a pencil and position it perpendicular to the cutting line.

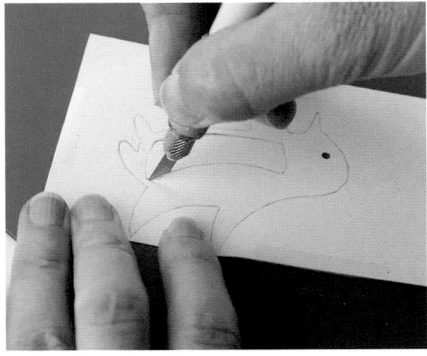

When it becomes difficult to cut, such as along curves or through many layers, hold the craft knife in a more upright position.

How to Cut Small Circles

OPTION #1: CUT WITH A CRAFT KNIFE

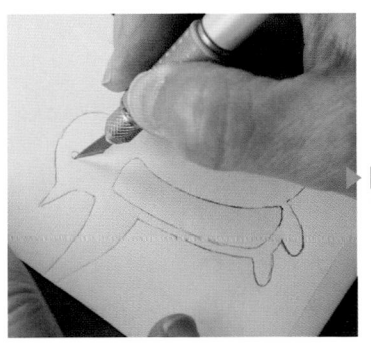 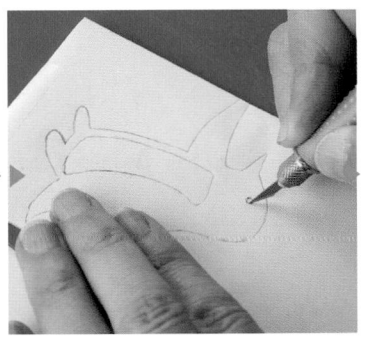 

Position the craft knife along the outline of the circle. Rotate the paper as you cut to create a nice, smooth circle.

OPTION #2: PUNCTURE WITH AN EYELETEER

An eyeleteer is a tool used to install eyelets. Without the eyelets, it serves as an excellent tool for punching holes in paper and is available in a wide variety of sizes.

Position the eyeleteer at a 90° angle along the outline of the circle. Press firmly to puncture a hole.

How to Glue Your Paper Cutting Designs

Spray adhesive is ideal for gluing your paper cutting designs because it evenly coats the paper without staining or wrinkling.

1. Arrange the paper cutting design on top of a piece of scrap paper with the wrong side facing up and spray with glue.

2. Carefully position the paper cutting design in place.

3. Secure the paper cutting design and remove any wrinkles by using a finger to gently smooth out the paper, working from the center outward.

HOW TO USE THIS BOOK

The following guide shows the step-by-step process for creating paper cutting designs. This process includes copying the template, folding the paper, cutting the design and unfolding the finished project. This guide used the Hearts design on page 100 as an example, but the basic construction techniques shown here apply to all projects in the book.

148 HEARTS (SHOWN ON PAGE 100)

Tools: Scissors
Folding Technique: Quadruple geometric fold

Mountain fold center

Full-Size Template Key

⬜ = Part to cut out
⬛ = Completed paper cutting design

Use the shading system listed above for all of the templates in this book.

Copy + Fold

1. Layer tracing paper on top of the template.

2. Using a ruler, trace the fold lines. Extend the lines slightly longer than the template outlines to preserve the correct angles.

Note: The fold lines are indicated in red in these diagrams.

3. With the fold lines aligned with the template outlines, trace the paper cutting design using a mechanical pencil. For neat lines, make sure to hold the paper in place while you trace.

4. Completed view of the copied template.

5. With the right side facing up, fold the paper in half to form a triangle.

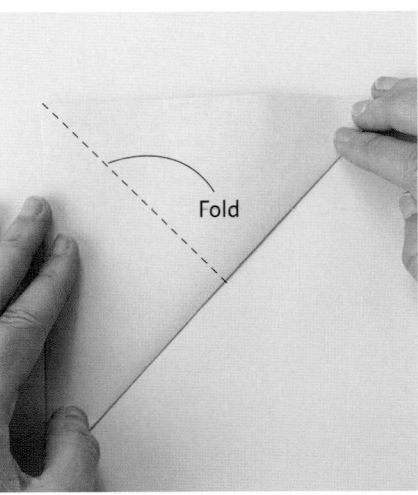

6. Fold the triangle in half again.

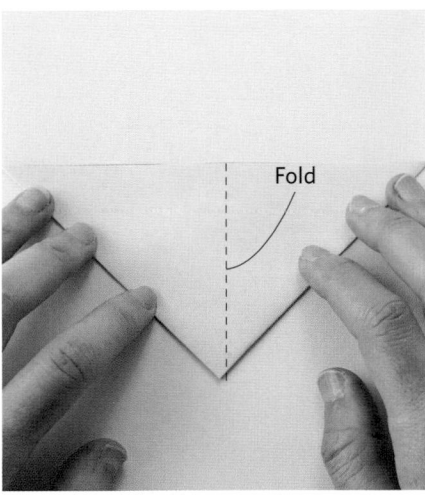

7. Fold the triangle in half once more.

8. Completed view of the quadruple geometric fold (refer to page 7 for detailed folding instructions).

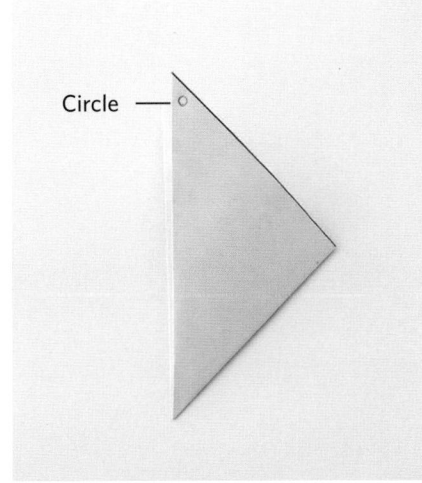

9. Mark the top of the triangle with a small circle. This circle will mark the top layer of paper, which will help you transfer the template to the correct section, then refold the paper for cutting.

10. Unfold the paper. Layer the tracing paper with copied template on the wrong side of your unfolded paper. Align the red fold lines on the tracing paper with the creases on the unfolded paper. Make sure the template is positioned on the section of paper with the circle.

11. Trace over the pencil lines on the tracing paper using a ballpoint pen. This will create indents in the paper. Hold the paper in place while you trace to prevent shifting.

12. Completed view of the template transferred to the folded paper.

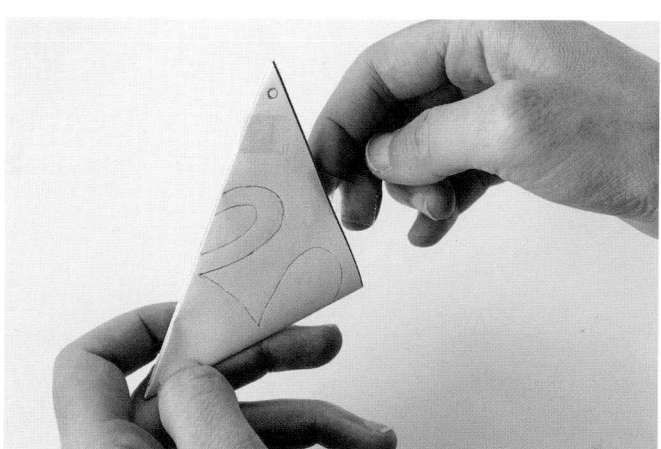

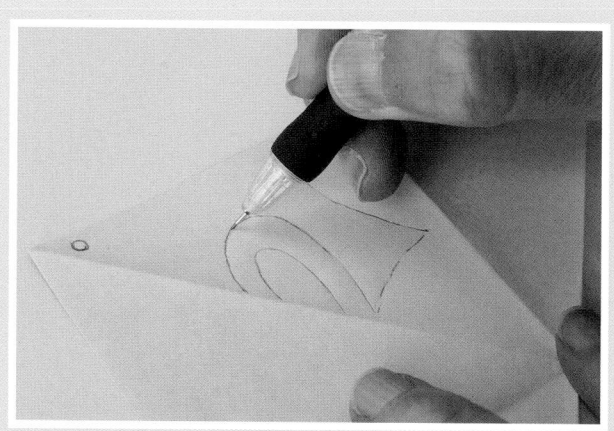

13. Refold the paper. Attach a piece of tape to hold the layers of paper together, making sure the tape doesn't cover the design.

If the indents are hard to see or if parts of the design are missing after using the ballpoint pen, it is helpful to retouch the lines with a mechanical pencil.

Cut

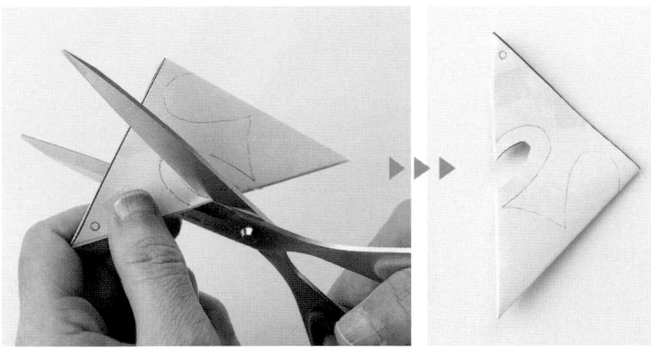

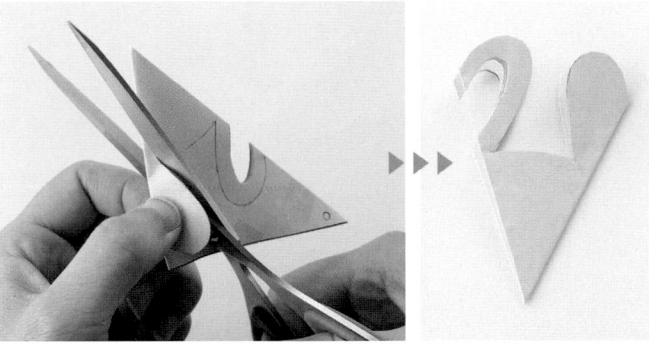

1. Cut out the part of the design along the fold (refer to page 11 for detailed cutting instructions).

2. Cut out the rest of the design.

Unfold

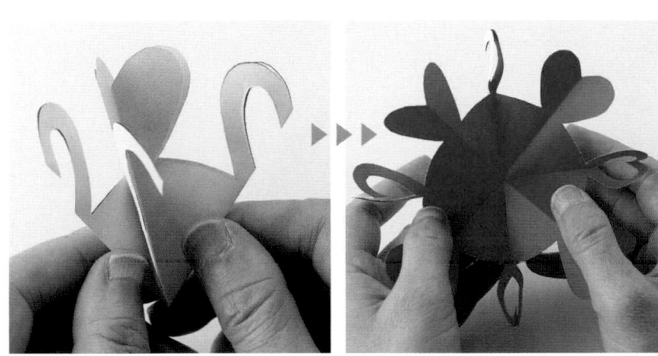

1. In order to prevent the paper from ripping, unfold it gently. The layers of paper may stick together, so work slowly.

2. Completed view of the paper cutting design.

WORLD LANDMARKS AND ICONS

1 Arc de Triomphe | **2** Eiffel Tower | **3** Poodle |
4 Carousel | *Templates on pages 20–21*

5 Tower Bridge | **6** Big Ben | **7** Terrier | **8** St. Paul's Cathedral | **9** Double-Decker Bus | *Templates on pages 22–23*

1 ARC DE TRIOMPHE

Tools: Scissors, craft knife
Folding Technique: Single geometric fold

Mountain fold ▶

Use craft knife →

Use craft knife

Use craft knife

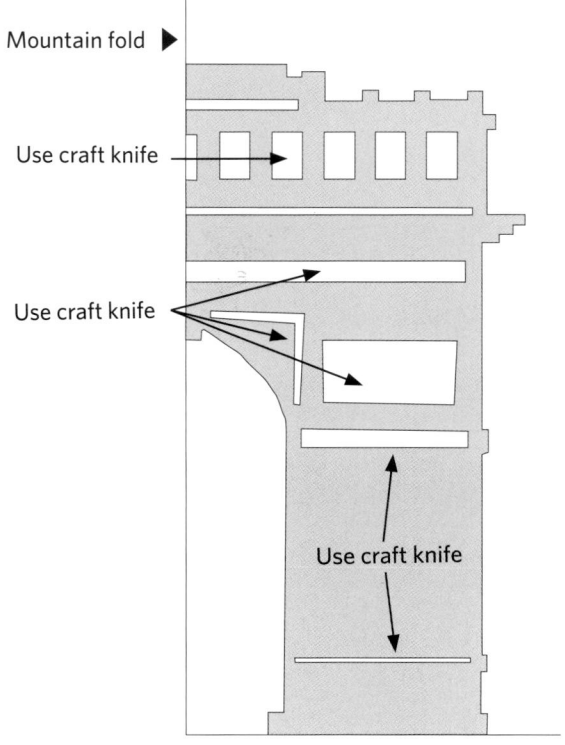

2 EIFFEL TOWER

Tools: Scissors
Folding Technique: Single geometric fold

Mountain fold ▶

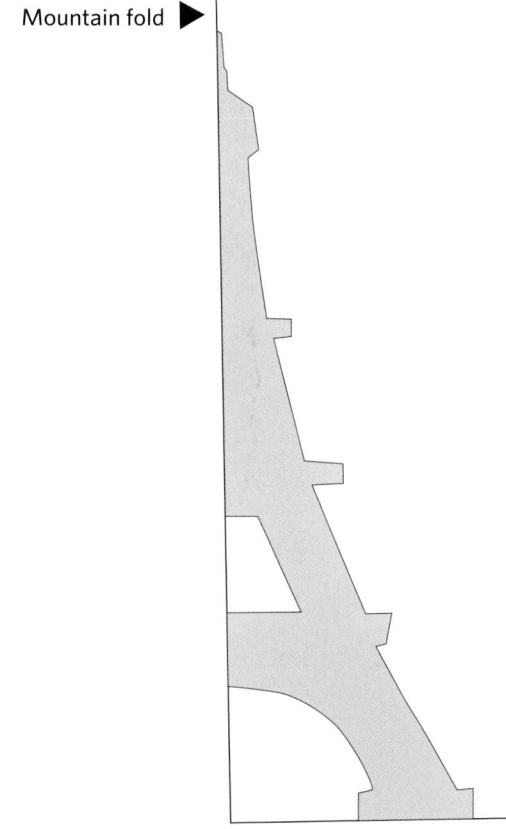

3 POODLE

Tools: Scissors, craft knife
Folding Technique: No fold

Use craft knife or eyeleteer to cut out the eye

Craft handmade cards for every occasion using paper cutting designs. For a special touch, use coordinating motifs to decorate the envelope.

4 CAROUSEL

Tools: Scissors, craft knife
Folding Technique: Triple geometric fold

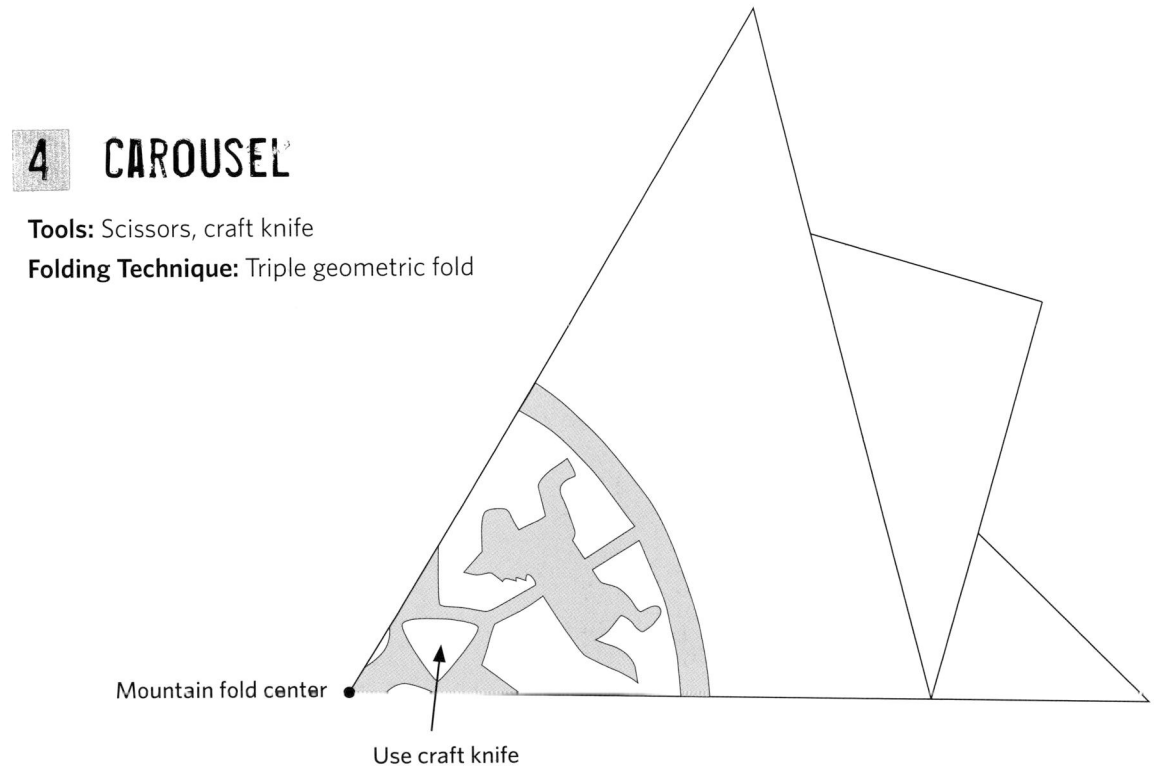

Mountain fold center

Use craft knife

5 TOWER BRIDGE

Tools: Scissors, craft knife
Folding Technique: Single geometric fold

Mountain fold ▶

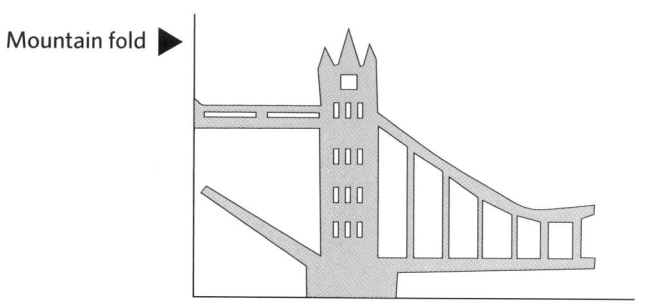

Use a craft knife to carefully cut out the windows and cables

6 BIG BEN

Tools: Scissors, craft knife
Folding Technique: Single geometric fold

Mountain fold ▶

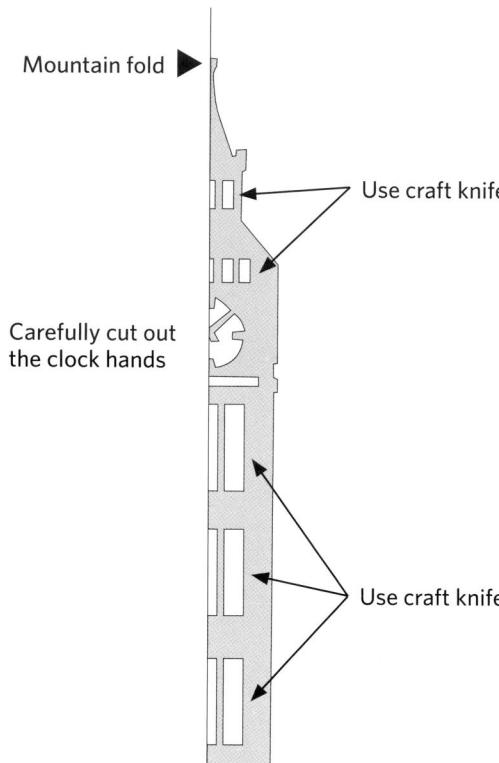

Use craft knife

Carefully cut out the clock hands

Use craft knife

7 TERRIER

Tools: Scissors, craft knife
Folding Technique: No fold

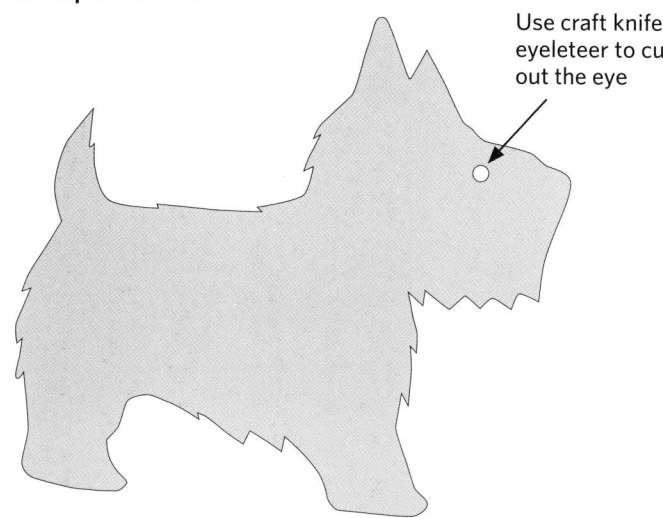

Use craft knife or eyeleteer to cut out the eye

8 ST. PAUL'S CATHEDRAL

Tools: Scissors, craft knife
Folding Technique: Single geometric fold

Mountain fold ▶

Use a craft knife to cut out all windows

Mountain fold ▶

Use a craft knife to cut out the windows and tire

9 DOUBLE-DECKER BUS

Tools: Scissors, craft knife
Folding Technique: Single geometric fold

Unfold the paper and cut out these two boxes on one side only

10 German Timbered House | **11** Scandinavian Log House | **12** Wooden Church | **13** Stained Glass | *Templates on pages 26–27*

14 Windmill | **15** Wooden Clogs | **16** Traditional Amsterdam Building | **17** Girl in Dutch Folk Costume | **18** Tulips | *Templates on pages 27–29*

10 GERMAN TIMBERED HOUSE

Tools: Scissors, craft knife
Folding Technique: Single geometric fold

Mountain fold ▶

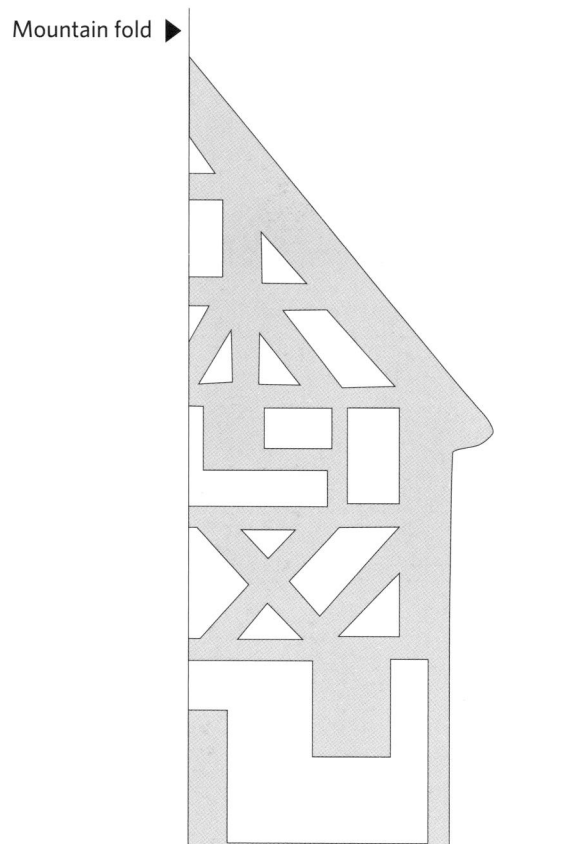

Use scissors to cut out the areas located on the mountain fold line and a craft knife for all other cuts

11 SCANDINAVIAN LOG HOUSE

Tools: Scissors, craft knife
Folding Technique: Single geometric fold

Mountain fold ▶

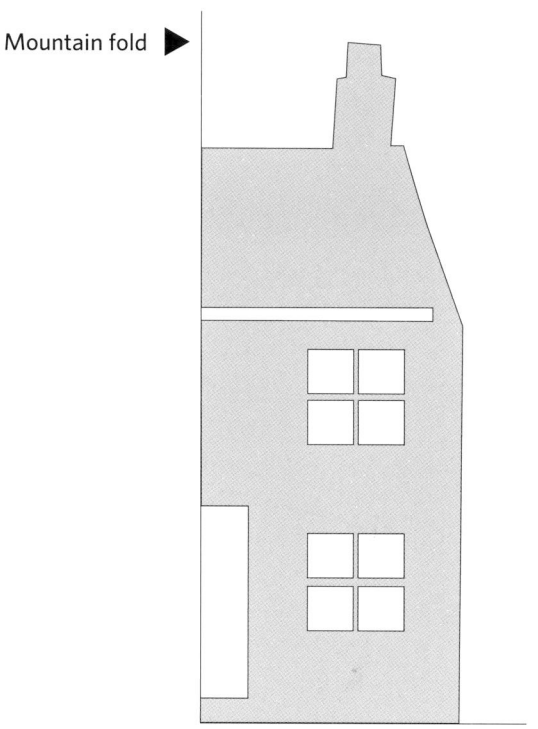

Use a craft knife to cut out the windows

Mountain fold ▶

12 WOODEN CHURCH

Tools: Scissors, craft knife
Folding Technique: Single geometric fold

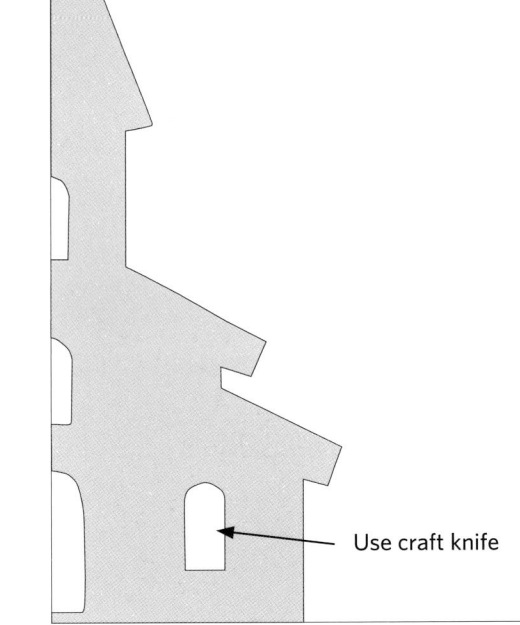

Use craft knife

13 STAINED GLASS

Tools: Scissors
Folding Technique: Sextuple geometric fold

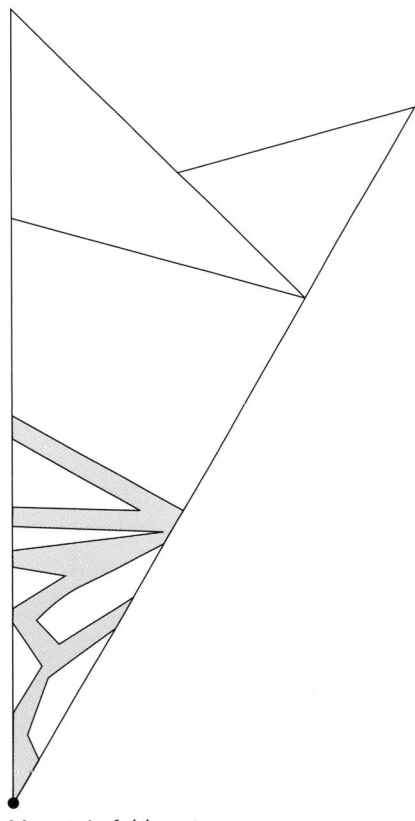

Mountain fold center

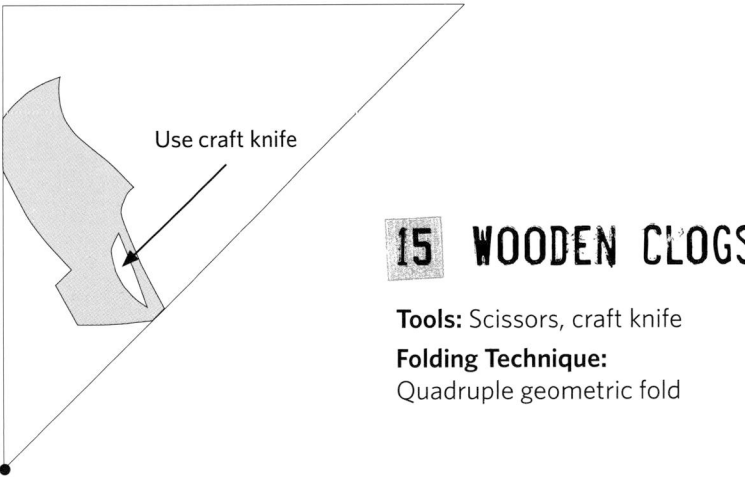

Use craft knife

Mountain fold center

15 WOODEN CLOGS

Tools: Scissors, craft knife
Folding Technique:
Quadruple geometric fold

14 WINDMILL

Tools: Scissors
Folding Technique: Single geometric fold

Mountain ▶
fold

18 TULIPS

Tools: Scissors
Folding Technique: Double accordion fold

Mountain fold ▶

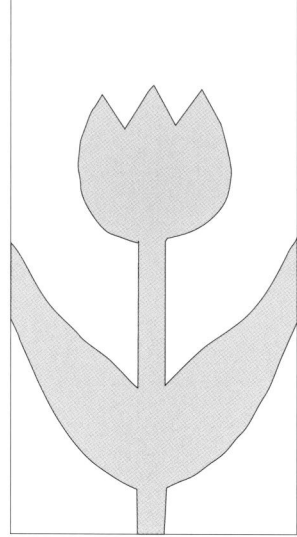

Create a work of art by combining two complementary motifs, such as the Windmill and Tulips. Simply glue the motifs to a piece of paper, then add a frame for a professional finish.

Mountain fold ▶

16 TRADITIONAL AMSTERDAM BUILDING

Tools: Scissors
Folding Technique: Single geometric fold

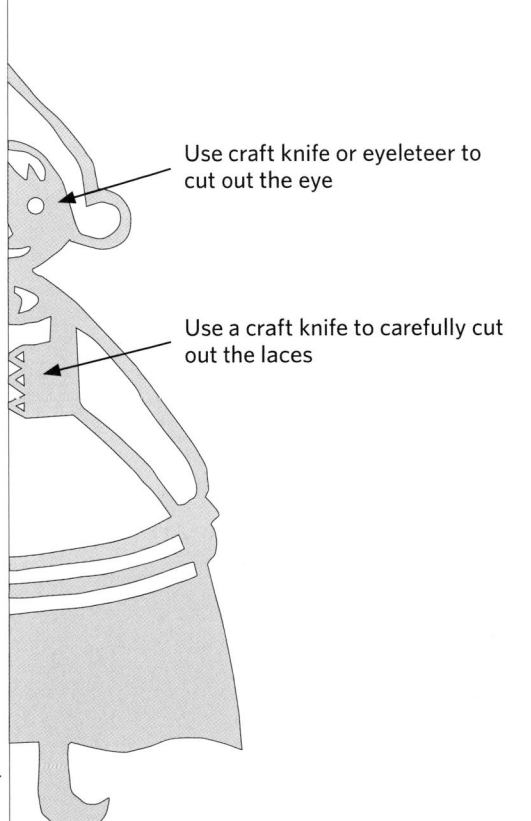

Use craft knife or eyeleteer to cut out the eye

Use a craft knife to carefully cut out the laces

17 GIRL IN DUTCH FOLK COSTUME

Tools: Scissors, craft knife
Folding Technique: Single geometric fold

Mountain fold ▶

19 Tower of Pisa | **20** Rialto Bridge | **21** Gondola |
Templates on pages 32–33

22 Parthenon | **23** Sphinx |
24 Russian Church |
Templates on pages 32–33

19 TOWER OF PISA

Tools: Scissors
Folding Technique: Single geometric fold

Mountain fold ▶

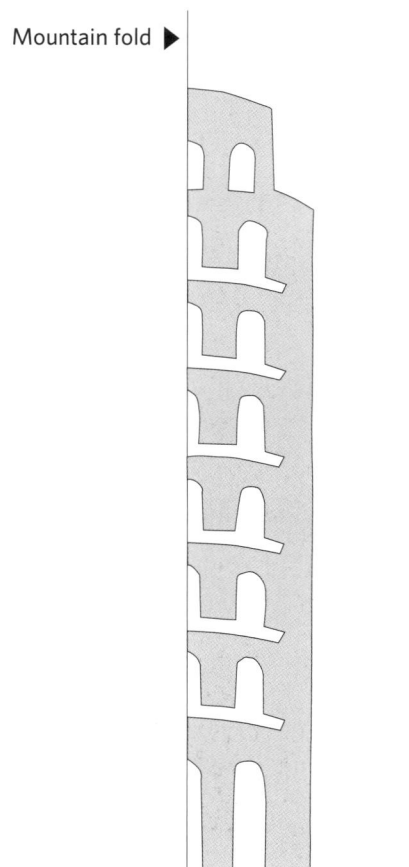

To make the tower lean, unfold and trim bottom at a slight angle

20 RIALTO BRIDGE

Tools: Scissors, craft knife
Folding Technique: Single geometric fold

Mountain fold ▶

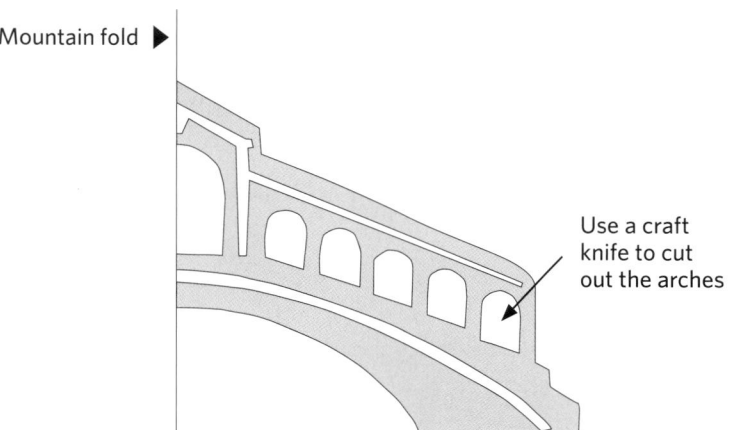

Use a craft knife to cut out the arches

22 PARTHENON

Tools: Scissors, craft knife
Folding Technique: Single geometric fold

Mountain fold ▶

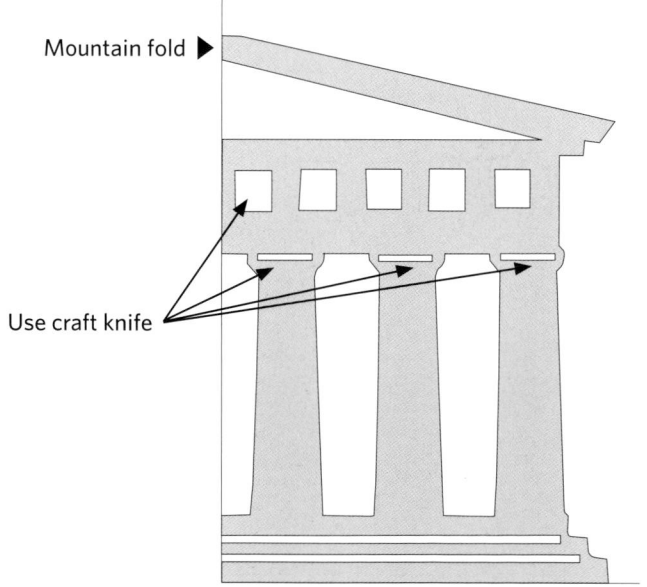

Use craft knife

21 GONDOLA

Tools: Scissors, craft knife
Folding Technique: No fold

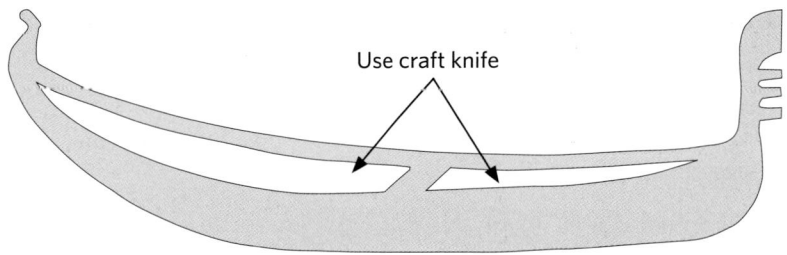

Use craft knife

24 RUSSIAN CHURCH

Tools: Scissors, craft knife
Folding Technique: Single geometric fold

23 SPHINX

Tools: Scissors, craft knife
Folding Technique: Single geometric fold

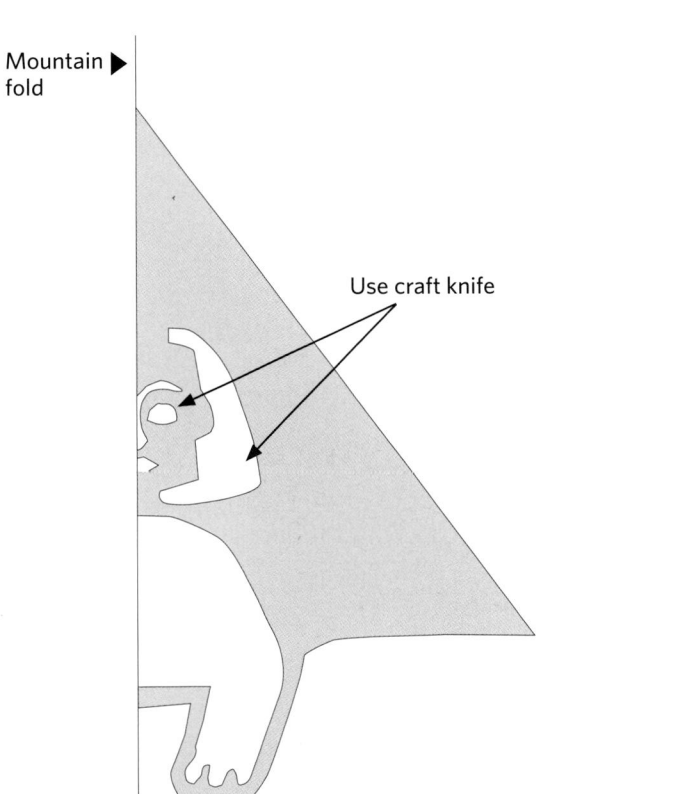

Mountain fold ▶

Use craft knife

Mountain fold ▶

Use scissors to cut out the areas located on the mountain fold line and a craft knife for all other cuts

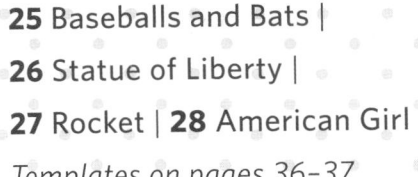

25 Baseballs and Bats |

26 Statue of Liberty |

27 Rocket | **28** American Girl |

Templates on pages 36–37

25

26

27

28

29

30

31

32

25 BASEBALLS AND BATS

Tools: Scissors, craft knife
Folding Technique: Quadruple accordion fold

Mountain fold ▶

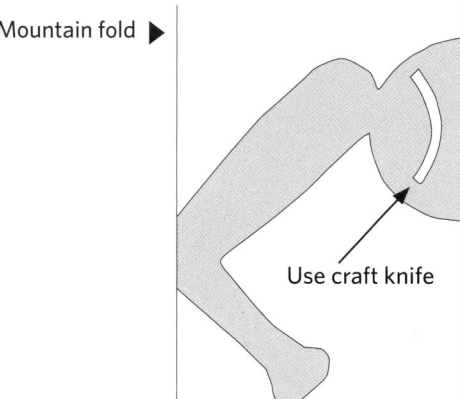

Use craft knife

Note: To make this project appear as shown on page 34, cut off the extra sections.

26 STATUE OF LIBERTY

Tools: Scissors, craft knife
Folding Technique: No fold

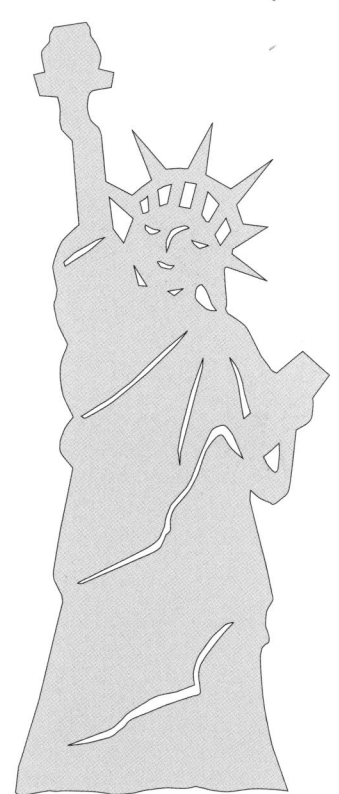

Use scissors for the outline and a craft knife for all other cuts

27 ROCKET

Tools: Scissors, craft knife
Folding Technique: Single geometric fold

Mountain fold ▶

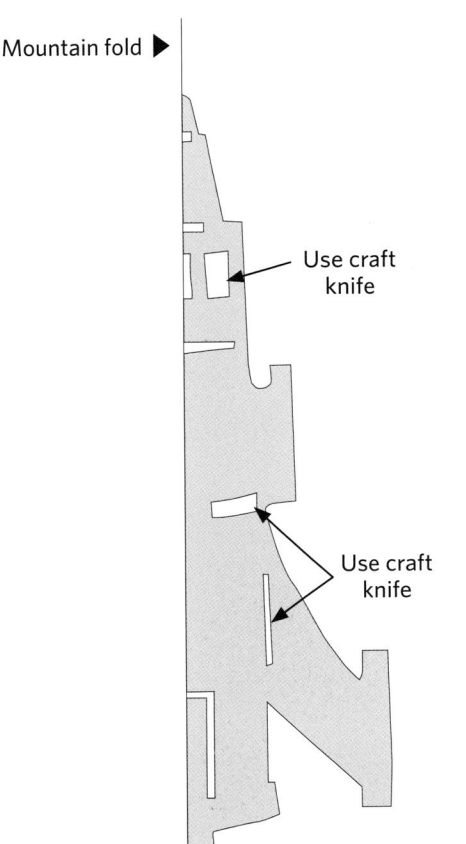

Use craft knife

Use craft knife

28 AMERICAN GIRL

Tools: Scissors, craft knife
Folding Technique: Single geometric fold

Mountain ▶ fold

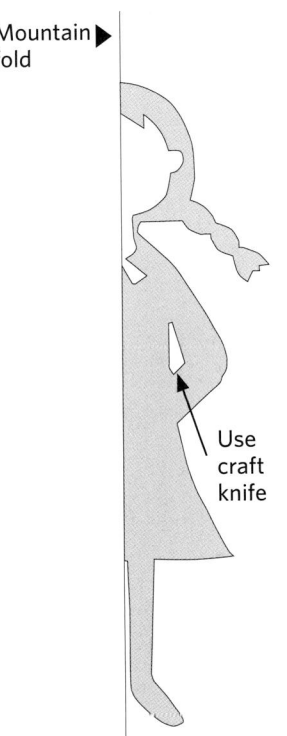

Use craft knife

29 MAPLE LEAVES

Tools: Scissors
Folding Technique: Sextuple geometric fold

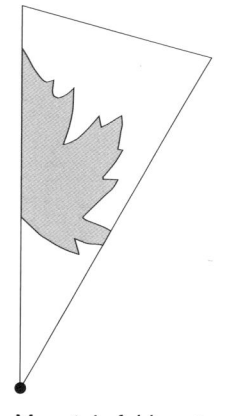

Mountain fold center

30 CONDORS

Tools: Scissors
Folding Technique: Quadruple geometric fold

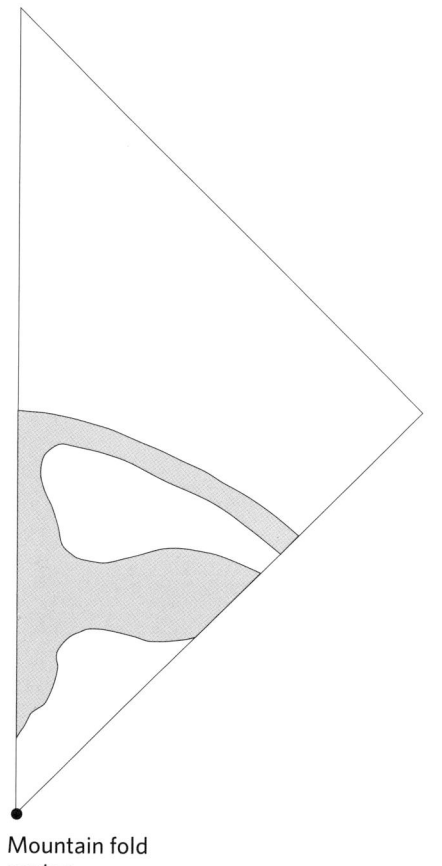

Mountain fold
center

31 SOMBRERO

Tools: Scissors
Folding Technique: Single geometric fold

Mountain fold ▶

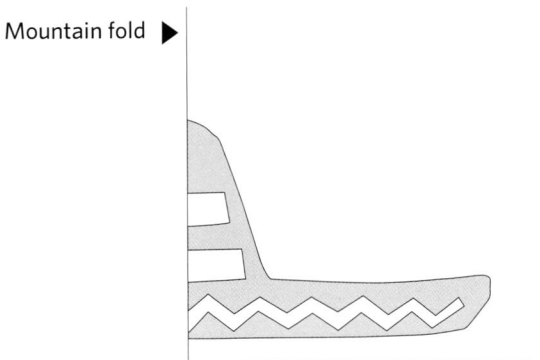

32 CACTUS

Tools: Scissors, craft knife
Folding Technique: Single geometric fold

Mountain fold ▶

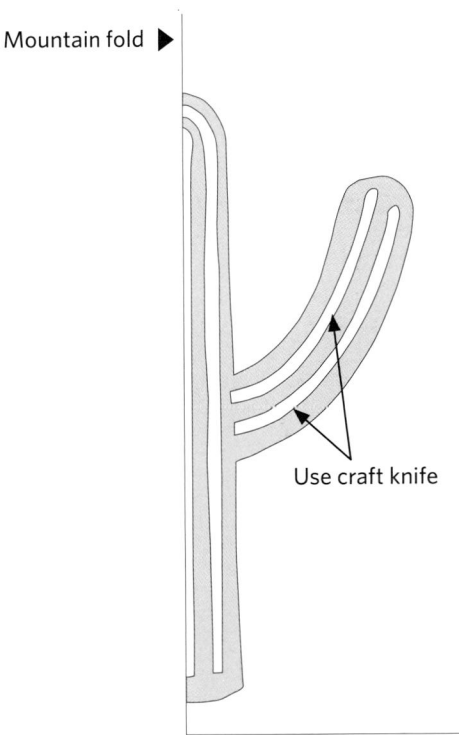

Use craft knife

33 Lantern | **34** Kaminarimon Gate | **35** Stone
Lantern | **36** Buddhist Monk | *Templates on pages 42–43*

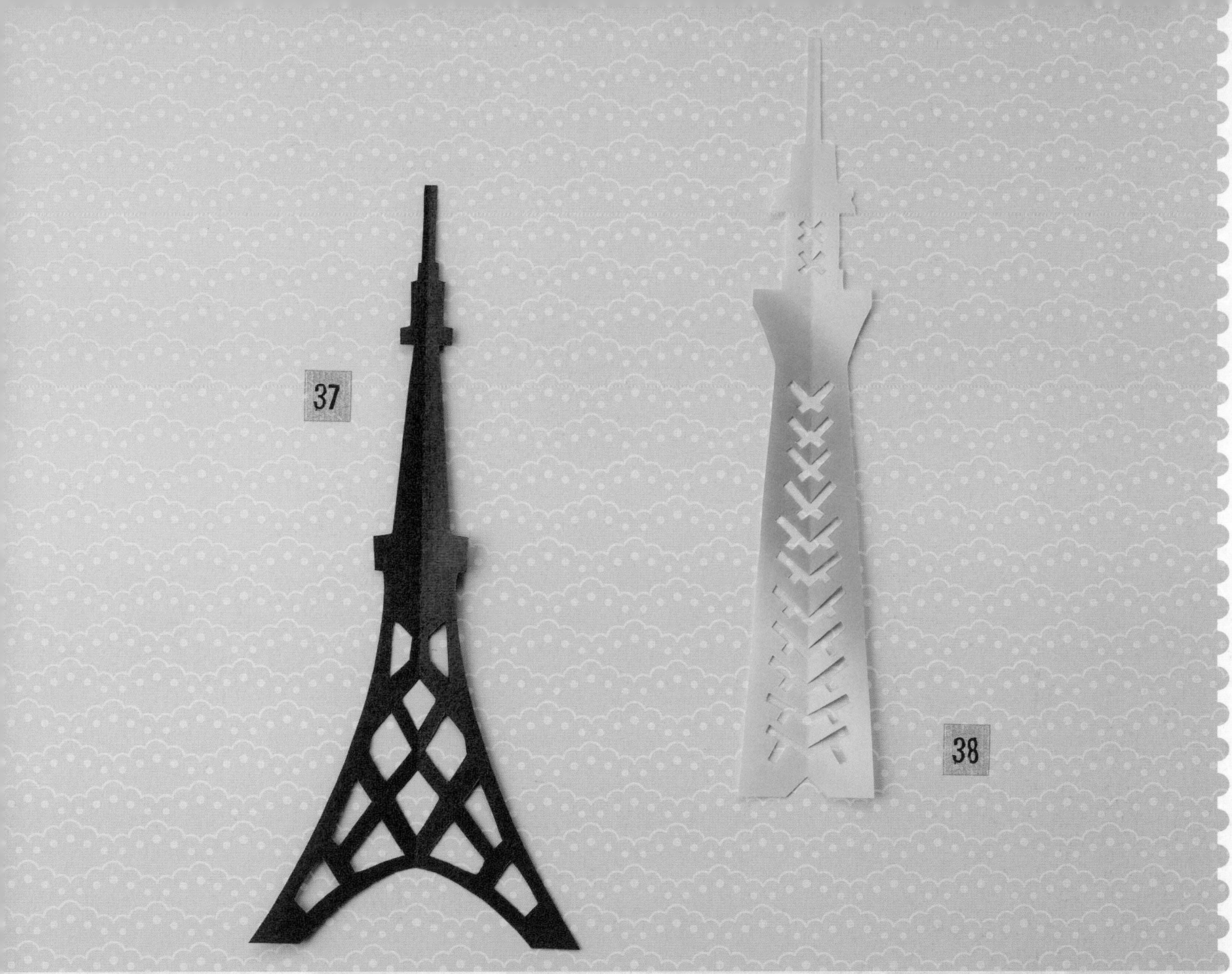

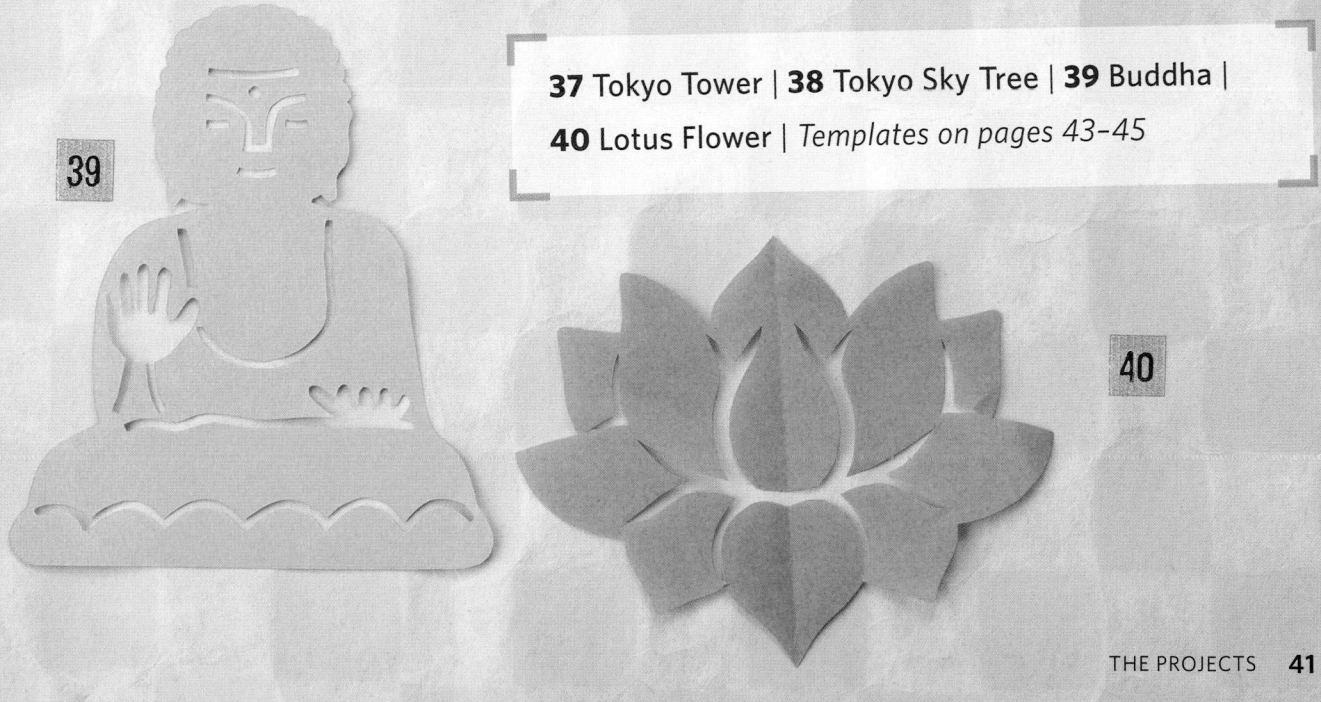

37 Tokyo Tower | **38** Tokyo Sky Tree | **39** Buddha |
40 Lotus Flower | *Templates on pages 43–45*

33 LANTERN

Tools: Scissors, craft knife
Folding Technique: Single geometric fold

Mountain fold ▶

Use craft knife

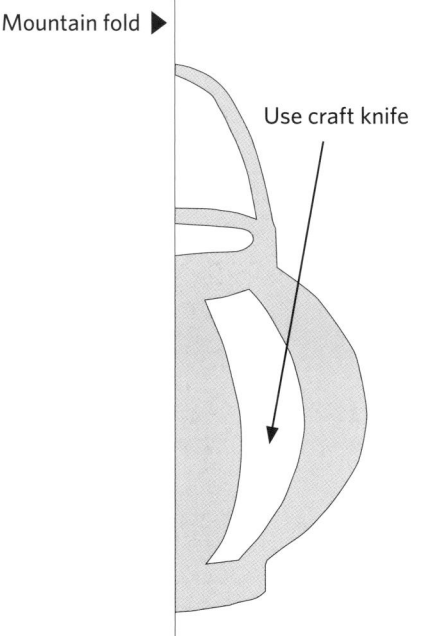

35 STONE LANTERN

Tools: Scissors
Folding Technique: Single geometric fold

Mountain fold ▶

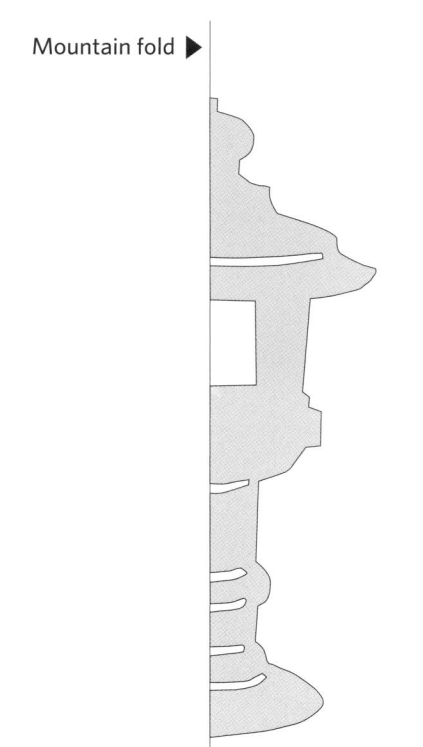

34 KAMINARIMON GATE

Tools: Scissors, craft knife
Folding Technique: Single geometric fold

Mountain fold ▶

Use craft knife

Use craft knife

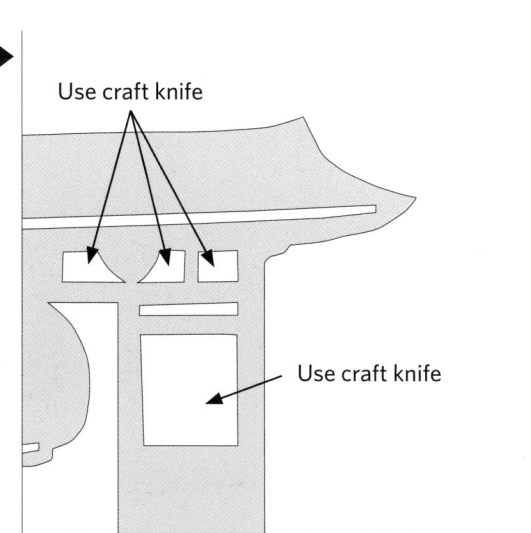

Mountain fold ▶

Use craft knife

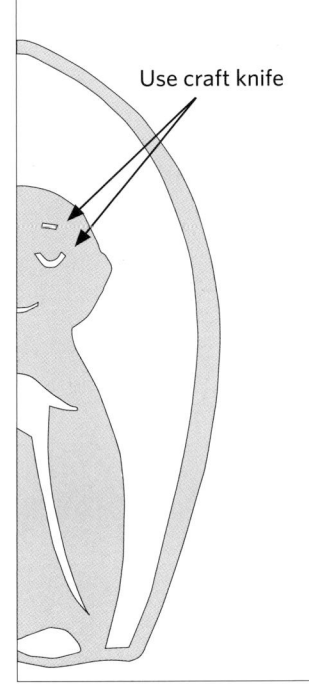

36 BUDDHIST MONK

Tools: Scissors, craft knife
Folding Technique: Single geometric fold

39 BUDDHA

Tools: Scissors, craft knife
Folding Technique: No fold

Use scissors for the outline and a craft knife for all other cuts

37 TOKYO TOWER

Tools: Scissors, craft knife
Folding Technique: Single geometric fold

Mountain fold ▶

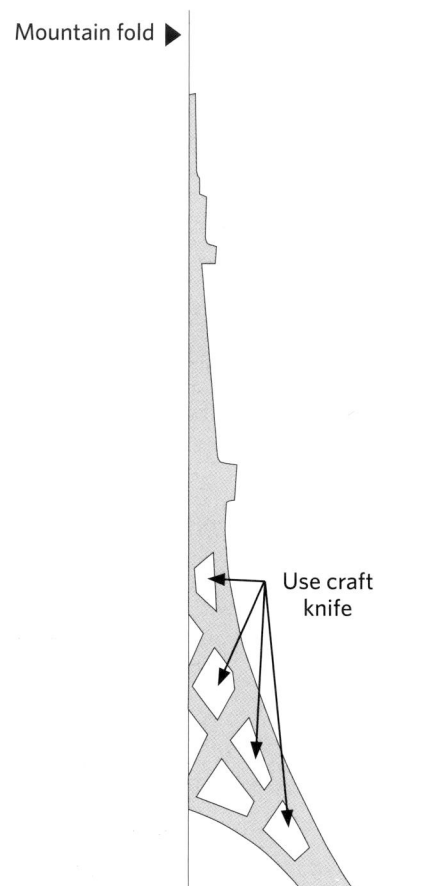

Use craft knife

38 TOKYO SKY TREE

Tools: Scissors
Folding Technique: Single geometric fold

Mountain fold ▶

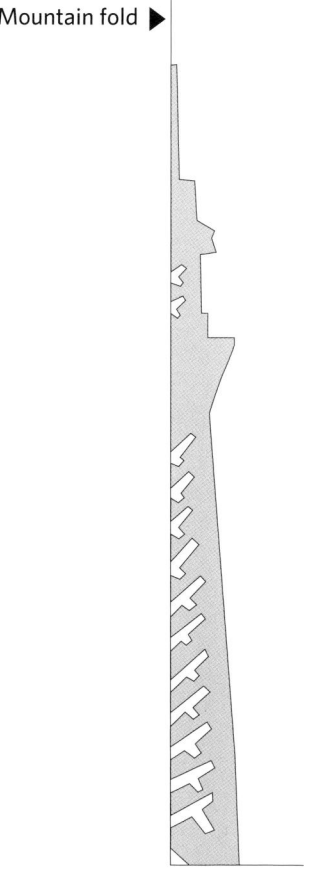

40 LOTUS FLOWER

Tools: Scissors, craft knife

Folding Technique: Single geometric fold

Mountain fold ▶

Use craft knife

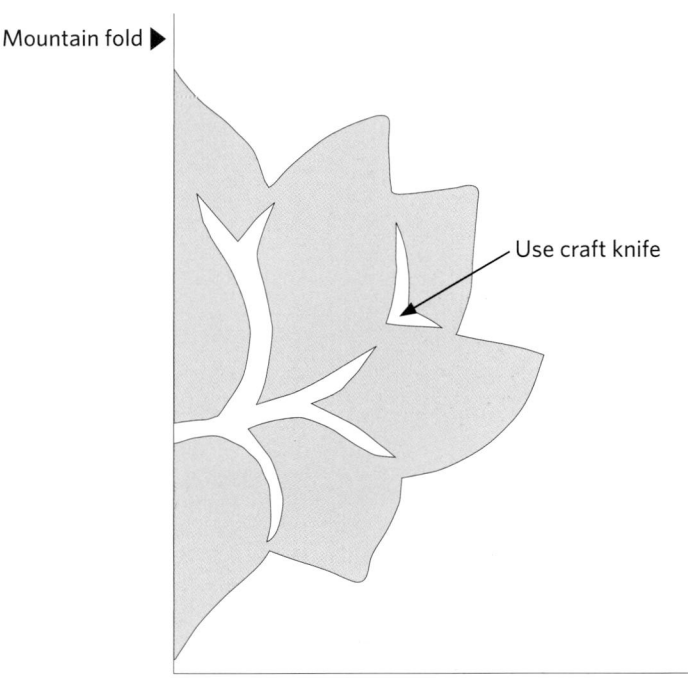

Create your own reflection journal by decorating the cover of a blank notebook with inspiring designs, such as the Lotus Flower, which is a Buddhist symbol of enlightenment.

41 Japanese Castle | **42** Pagoda | **43** Taj Mahal | **44** Chinese Key Pattern |
45 Double Happiness Symbol | **46** Gate of China | **47** Temple of Heaven |

Templates on pages 48–49

41 JAPANESE CASTLE

Tools: Scissors, craft knife
Folding Technique: Single geometric fold

Mountain fold ▶

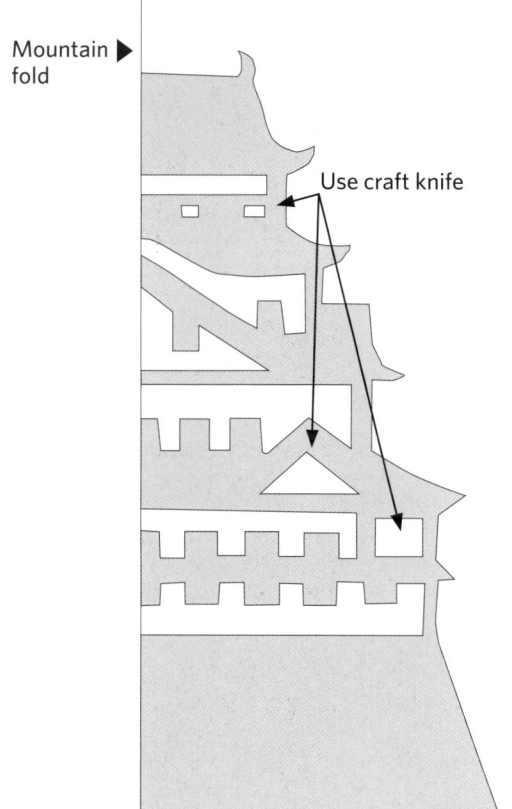

Mountain fold

Use craft knife

42 PAGODA

Tools: Scissors, craft knife
Folding Technique:
Single geometric fold

Use craft knife

43 TAJ MAHAL

Tools: Scissors, craft knife
Folding Technique: Single geometric fold

Mountain fold ▶

Use a craft knife to cut out all windows

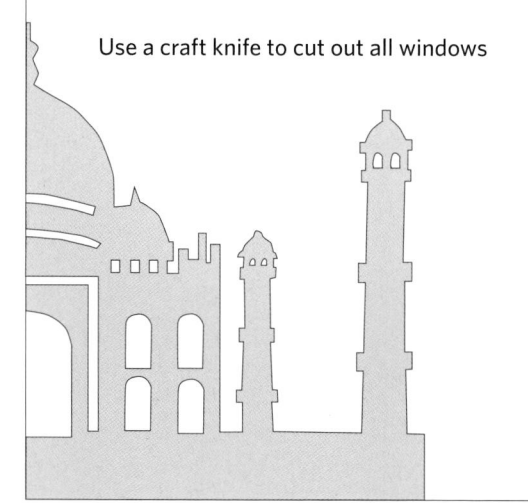

44 CHINESE KEY PATTERN

Tools: Scissors
Folding Technique: No fold

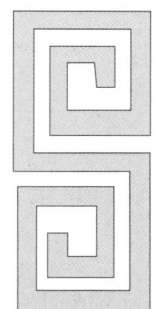

45 DOUBLE HAPPINESS SYMBOL

Tools: Scissors, craft knife
Folding Technique: Single geometric fold

Mountain fold ▶

Use craft knife →

Use craft knife

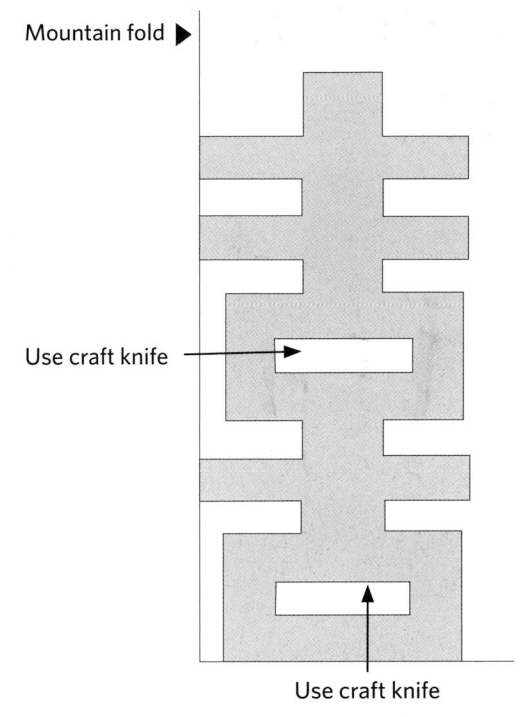

46 GATE OF CHINA

Tools: Scissors
Folding Technique: Single geometric fold

Mountain fold ▶

47 TEMPLE OF HEAVEN

Tools: Scissors, craft knife
Folding Technique: Single geometric fold

Mountain fold ▶

Use craft knife

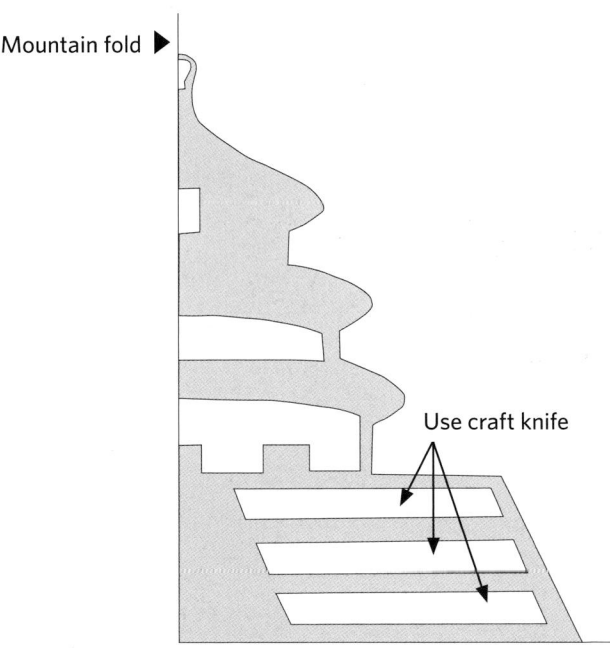

52 Butterfly | **53** Berry Border | **54** Flower Border | **55** Leaf Border | **56** Tribal Butterfly | *Templates on pages 54–55*

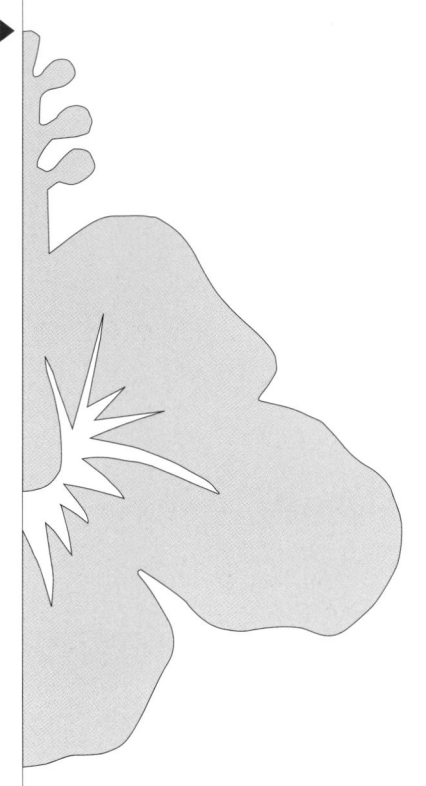

Mountain fold ▶

48 HIBISCUS FLOWER

Tools: Scissors
Folding Technique: Single geometric fold

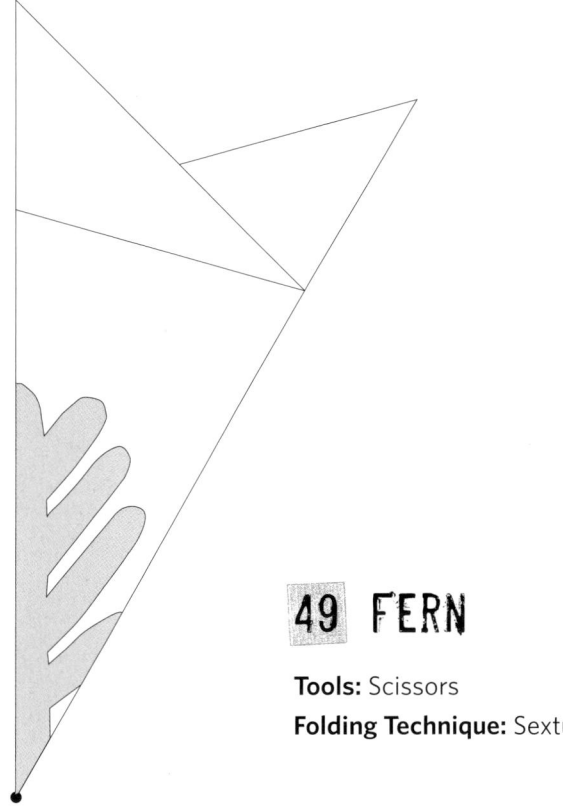

49 FERN

Tools: Scissors
Folding Technique: Sextuple geometric fold

Mountain fold center

50 PINEAPPLES

Tools: Scissors
Folding Technique: Quadruple geometric fold

Mountain fold center

Mountain fold ▶

Use craft knife

51 UKULELE

Tools: Scissors, craft knife
Folding Technique: Single geometric fold

Mountain fold ▶

52 BUTTERFLY

Tools: Scissors
Folding Technique: Single geometric fold

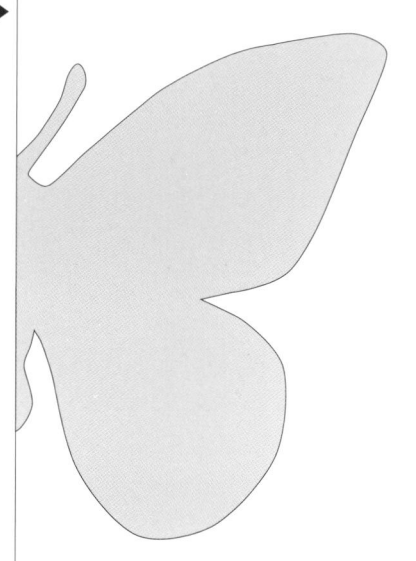

Mountain fold ▶

56 TRIBAL BUTTERFLY

Tools: Scissors, craft knife
Folding Technique: Single geometric fold

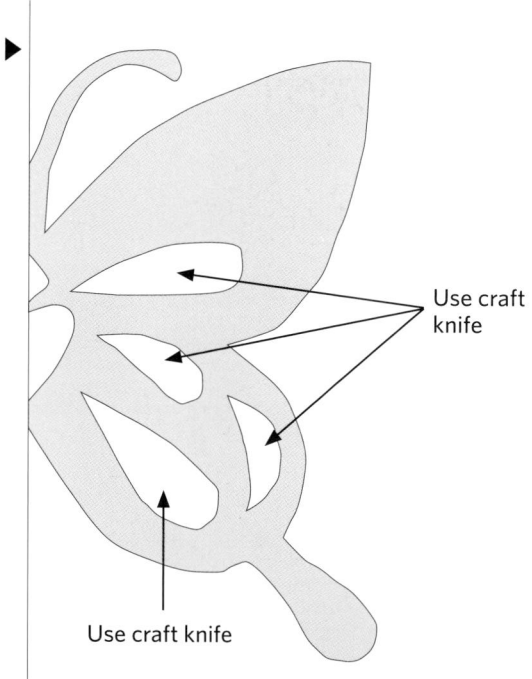

Use craft knife

Use craft knife

53 BERRY BORDER

Tools: Scissors
Folding Technique: Double accordion fold

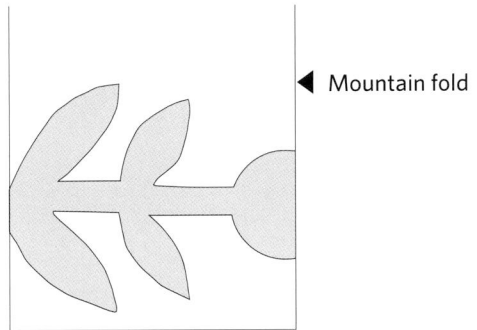

◀ Mountain fold

54 FLOWER BORDER

Tools: Scissors
Folding Technique: Double accordion fold

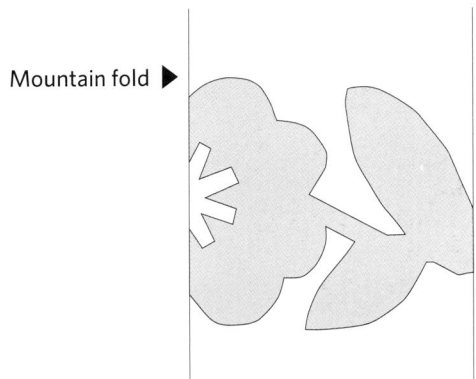

Mountain fold ▶

55 LEAF BORDER

Tools: Scissors
Folding Technique: Double accordion fold

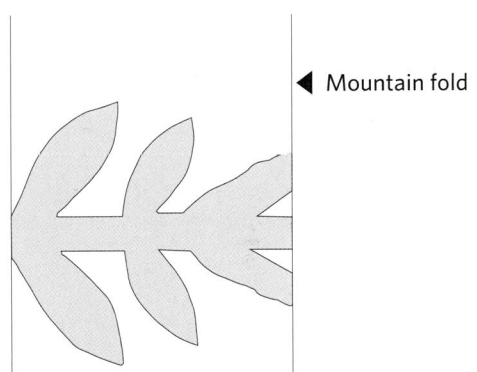

◀ Mountain fold

Glue borders to paper bags to create custom-designed gift wrap. These bags are great for presents, party favors or even a special lunch bag.

57 Coffee Plant | **58** Beach Umbrella | **59** Desert Island | **60** Palm Tree | *Templates on pages 58–59*

61 Angelfish | **62** Conch Shell | **63** Sea Turtles |
64 Dolphin | *Templates on pages 60–61*

61

62

64

63

57 COFFEE PLANT

Tools: Scissors
Folding Technique: Single geometric fold

Mountain fold ▶

Mountain fold ▶

58 BEACH UMBRELLA

Tools: Scissors
Folding Technique: Single geometric fold

59 DESERT ISLAND

Tools: Scissors, craft knife
Folding Technique: Single geometric fold

Mountain fold ▶

Use craft knife

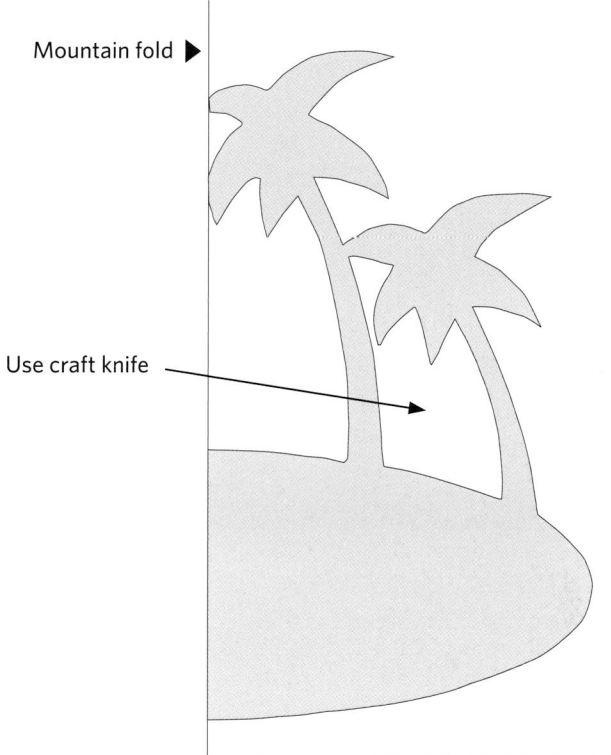

Mountain fold ▶

60 PALM TREE

Tools: Scissors
Folding Technique: Single geometric fold

61 | ANGELFISH

Tools: Scissors, craft knife
Folding Technique: No fold

Use scissors for the outline and a craft knife for all other cuts

62 | CONCH SHELL

Tools: Scissors, craft knife
Folding Technique: No fold

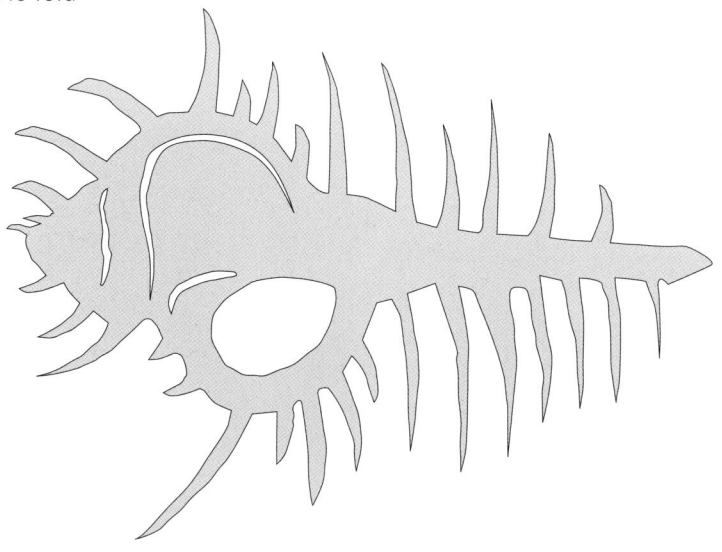

Use scissors for the outline and a craft knife for all other cuts

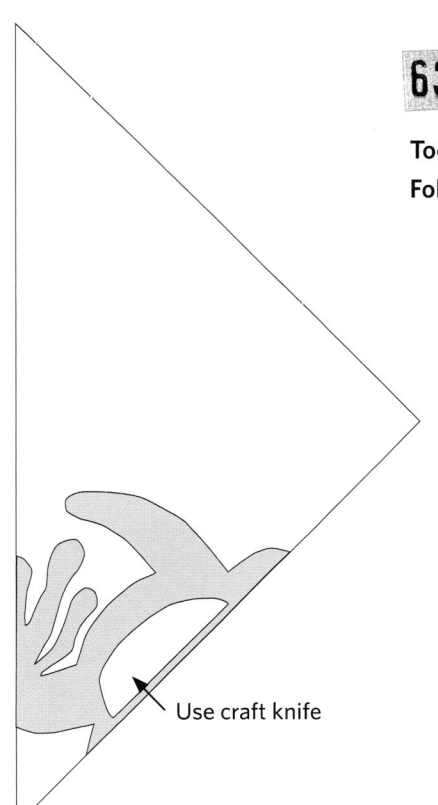

Use craft knife

Mountain fold center

63 SEA TURTLES

Tools: Scissors, craft knife
Folding Technique: Quadruple geometric fold

64 DOLPHIN

Tools: Scissors, craft knife
Folding Technique: No fold

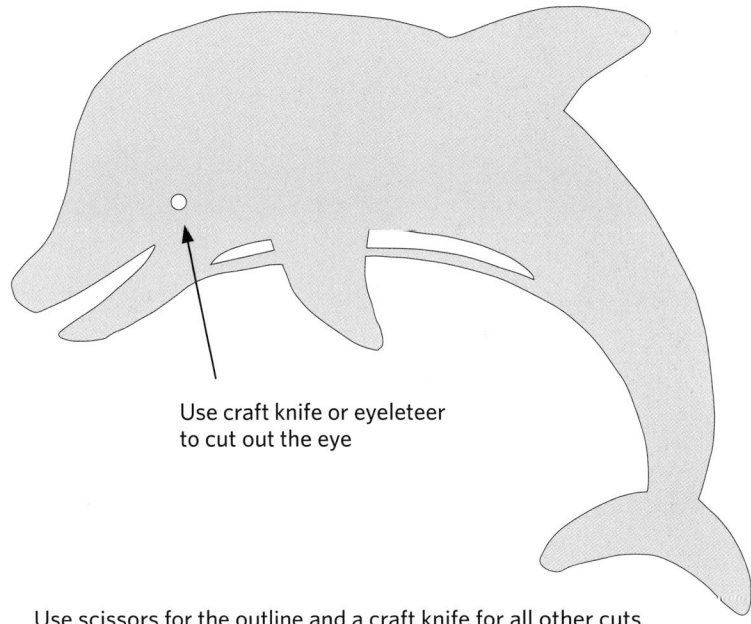

Use craft knife or eyeleteer
to cut out the eye

Use scissors for the outline and a craft knife for all other cuts

FOODS OF THE WORLD

65 Sausages | 66 Beer | 67 Baguette |
68 Wine Glass | 69 Wine Bottle |
Templates on pages 64–65

70 Pretzels | **71** Cupcake | **72** Ice Cream Cone | **73** Waffle | **74** Teacup | **75** Teapot | *Templates on pages 65–67*

65 SAUSAGES

Tools: Scissors
Folding Technique: Single geometric fold

Mountain fold ▶

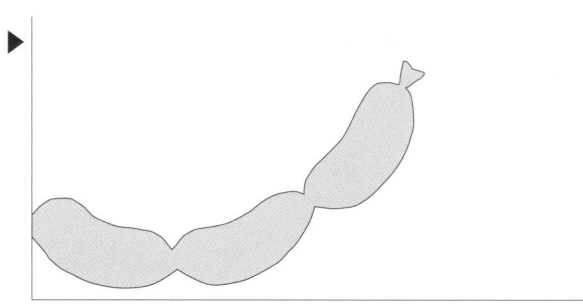

Mountain
fold ▶

66 BEER

Tools: Scissors, craft knife
Folding Technique: Single geometric fold

Unfold and cut the
handle out on one
side only

Use craft knife

67 BAGUETTE

Tools: Scissors
Folding Technique: No fold

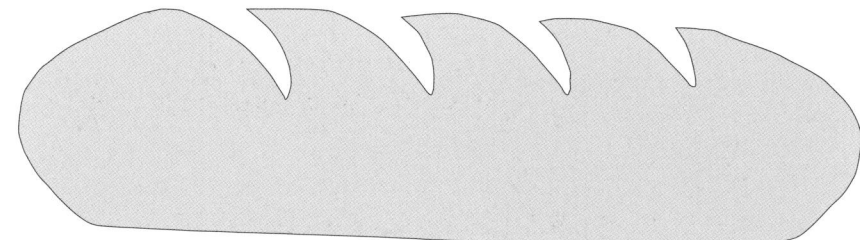

68 WINE GLASS

Tools: Scissors
Folding Technique: Single geometric fold

69 WINE BOTTLE

Tools: Scissors
Folding Technique: Single geometric fold

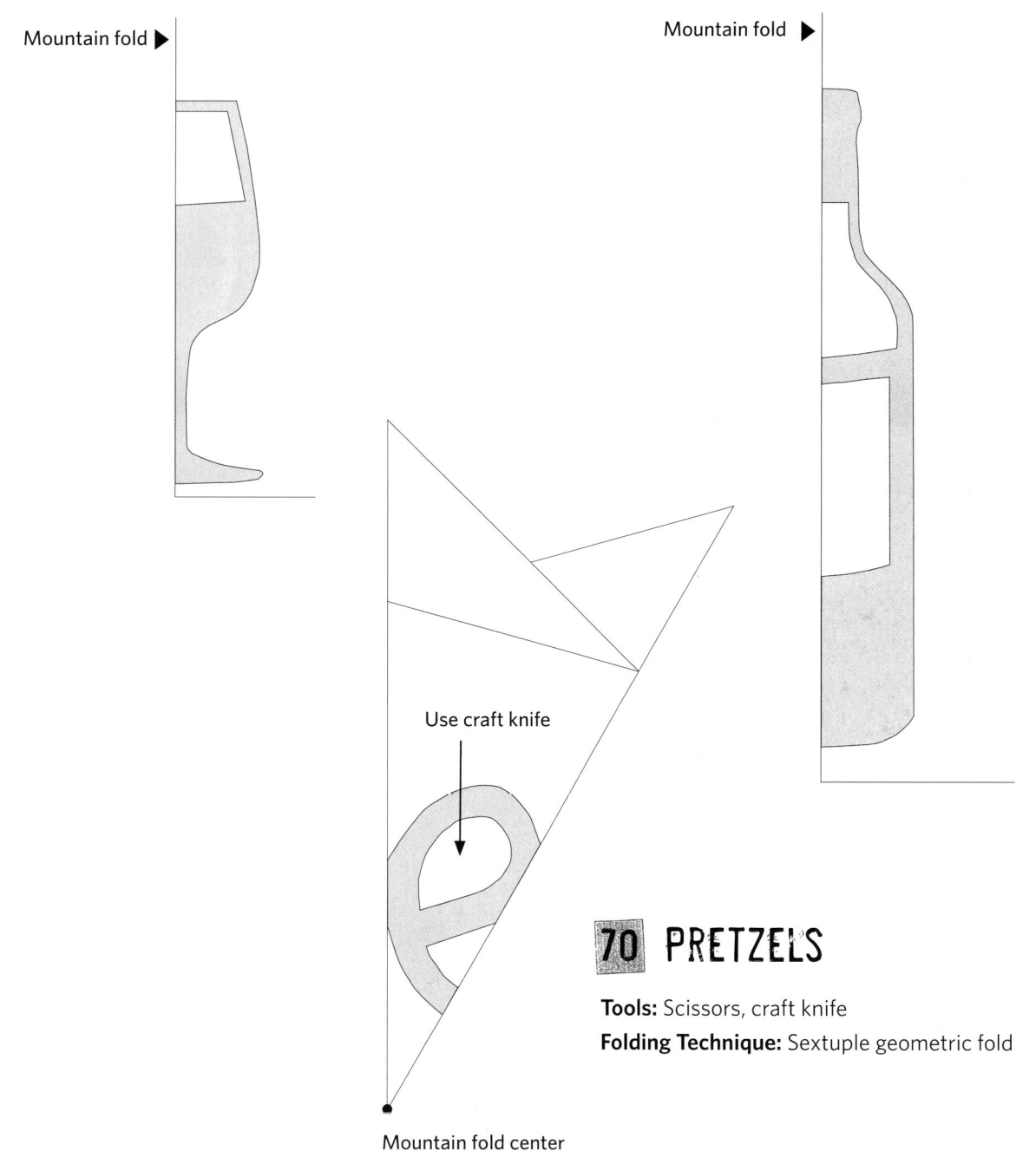

Mountain fold ▶

Mountain fold ▶

Use craft knife

Mountain fold center

70 PRETZELS

Tools: Scissors, craft knife
Folding Technique: Sextuple geometric fold

71 CUPCAKE

Tools: Scissors, craft knife, eyeleteer
Folding Technique: No fold

72 ICE CREAM CONE

Tools: Scissors, craft knife
Folding Technique: No fold

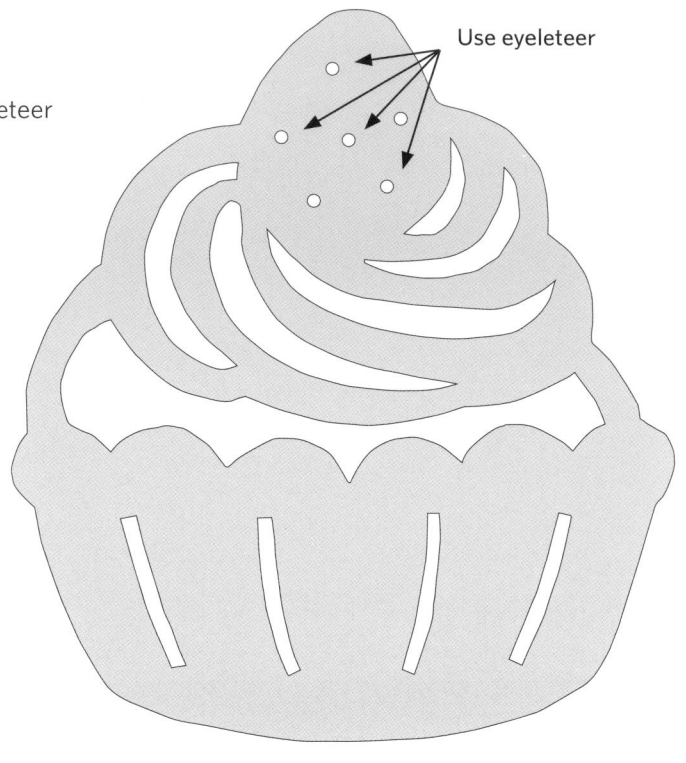

Use eyeleteer

Use scissors for the outline and a craft knife for all other cuts

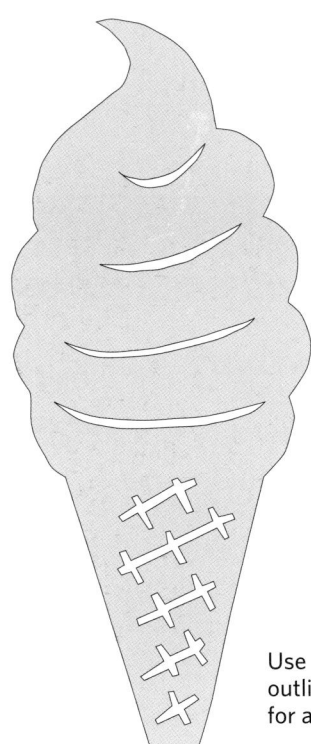

Use scissors for the outline and a craft knife for all other cuts

73 WAFFLE

Tools: Scissors, craft knife
Folding Technique: Single geometric fold

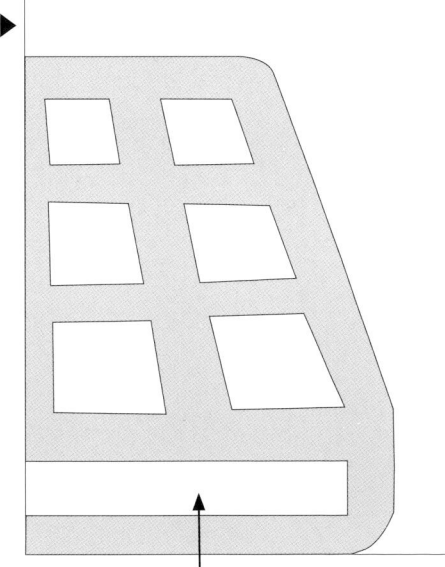

Mountain fold ▶

Use scissors for the outline and this section and a craft knife for all other cuts

74 TEACUP

Tools: Scissors, craft knife
Folding Technique: No fold

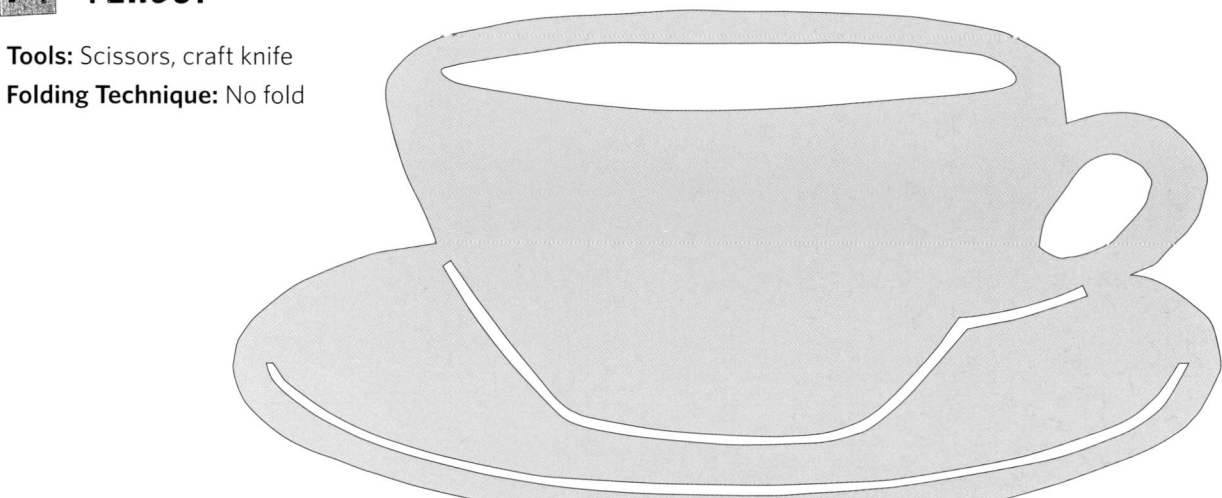

Use scissors for the outline and a craft knife for all other cuts

75 TEAPOT

Tools: Scissors, craft knife
Folding Technique: No fold

Use scissors for the outline and a craft knife for all other cuts

THE ANIMAL KINGDOM

76 Pandas | **77** Bamboo | **78** Llama | **79** Sheep |
Templates on pages 70–71

80 Kangaroo | **81** Camel |
82 Seal | **83** Otters |
Templates on pages 72–73

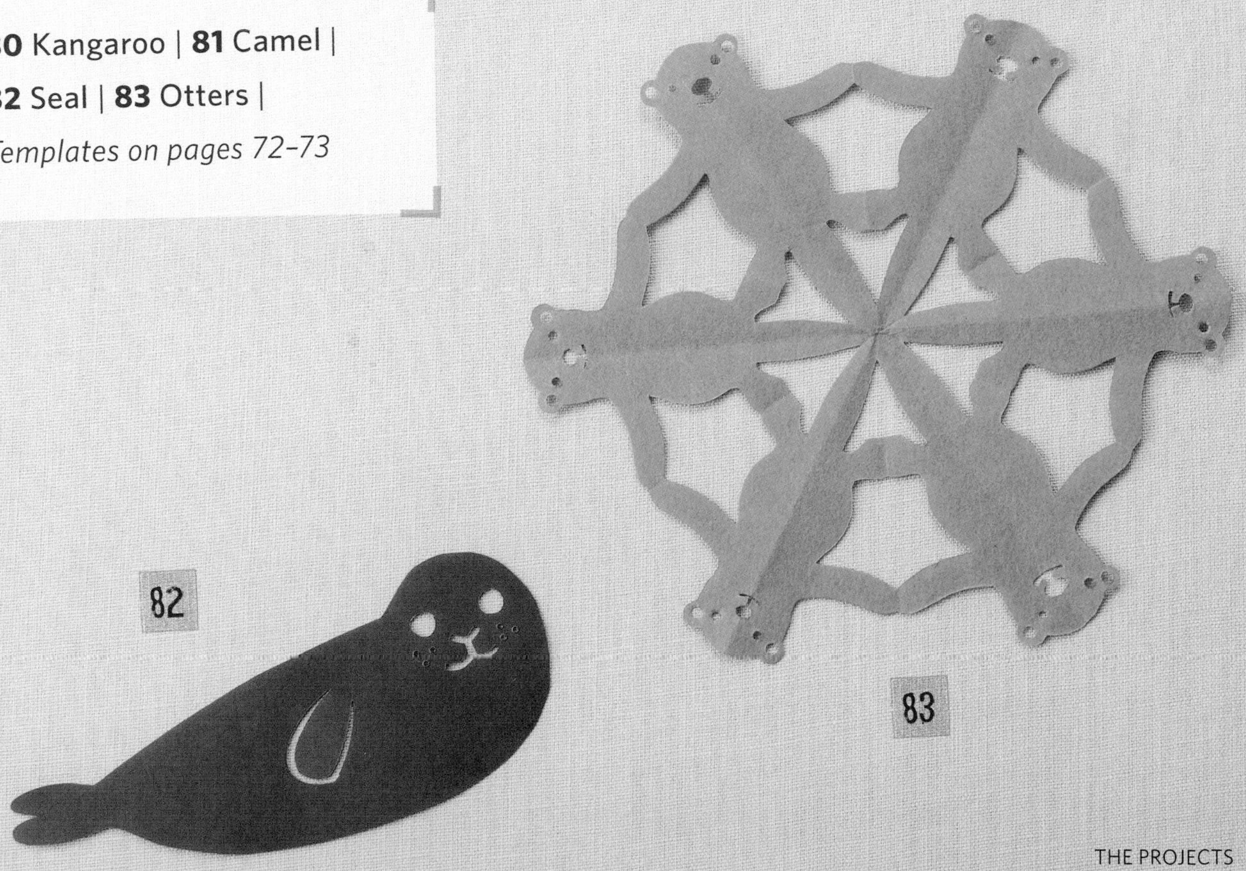

76 PANDAS

Tools: Scissors, craft knife
Folding Technique: Single geometric fold

Mountain ▶
fold

Use scissors for the outline and a craft knife for all other cuts

Decorate your notebook cover with these fun friends for one-of-a-kind school supplies.

77 BAMBOO

Tools: Scissors
Folding Technique: Single geometric fold

Mountain fold ▶

78 LLAMA

Tools: Scissors, craft knife
Folding Technique: No fold

Use scissors for the outline and a craft knife for all other cuts

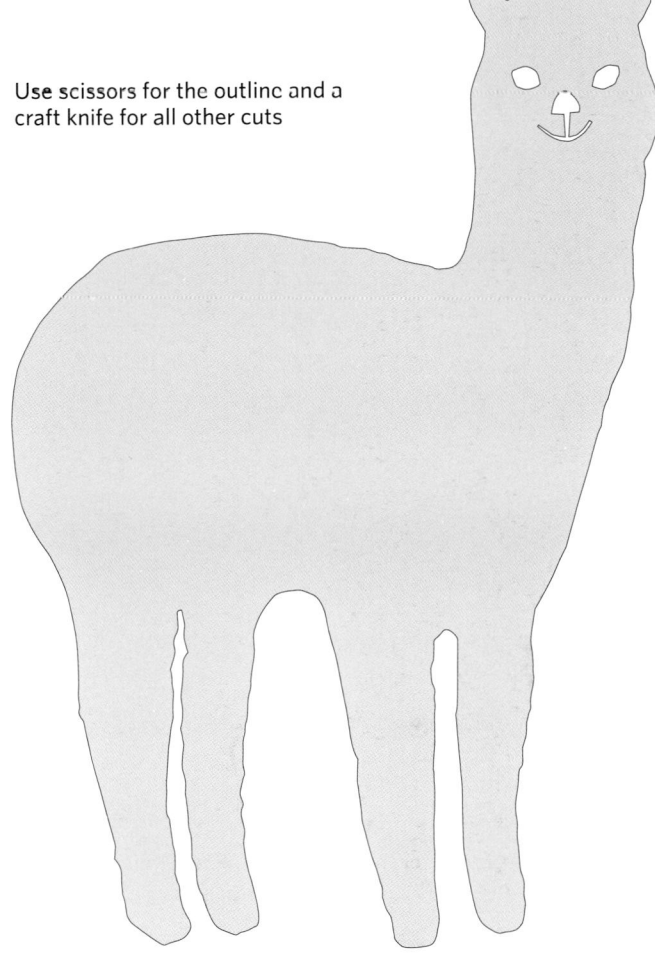

79 SHEEP

Tools: Scissors, craft knife, eyeleteer
Folding Technique: Single geometric fold

Mountain fold ▶

Use eyeleteer

Use craft knife

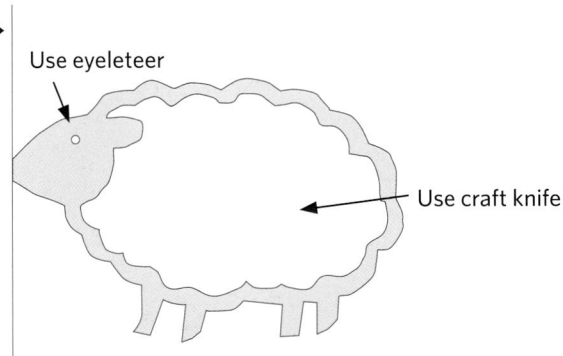

80 KANGAROO

Tools: Scissors, craft knife
Folding Technique: No fold

Use craft knife or eyeleteer to cut out the eyes

81 CAMEL

Tools: Scissors, craft knife
Folding Technique: No fold

Use craft knife or eyeleteer to cut out the eye

82 SEAL

Tools: Scissors, craft knife, eyeleteer
Folding Technique: No fold

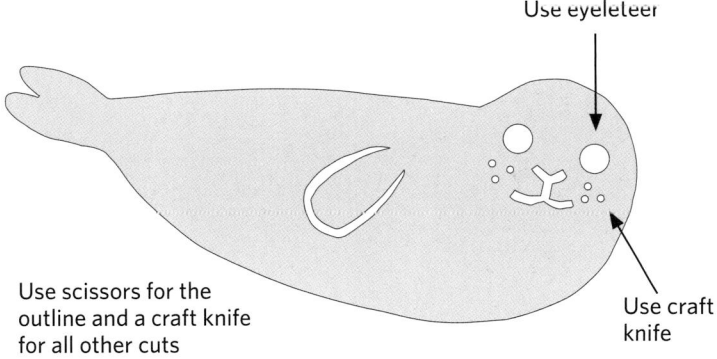

Use eyeleteer

Use scissors for the outline and a craft knife for all other cuts

Use craft knife

83 OTTERS

Tools: Scissors, craft knife
Folding Technique: Sextuple geometric fold

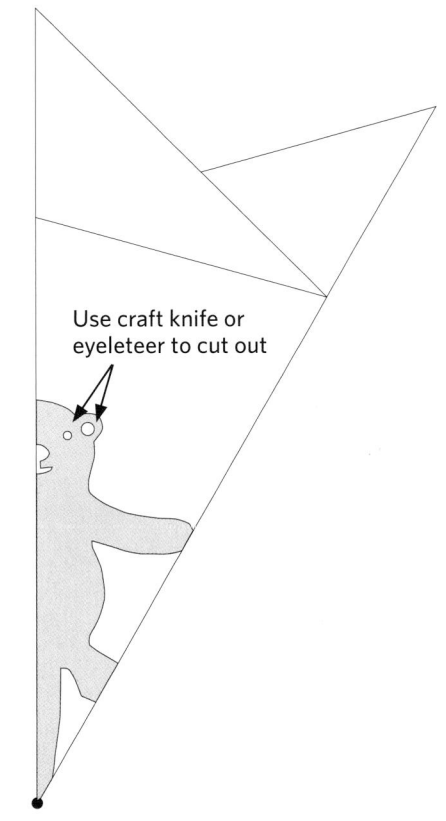

Use craft knife or eyeleteer to cut out

Mountain fold center

84 Elephant | **85** Hippopotamus | **86** Zebra |
87 Grass | *Templates on pages 76–77*

88

89

90

91

84 ELEPHANT

Tools: Scissors, craft knife, eyeleteer
Folding Technique: No fold

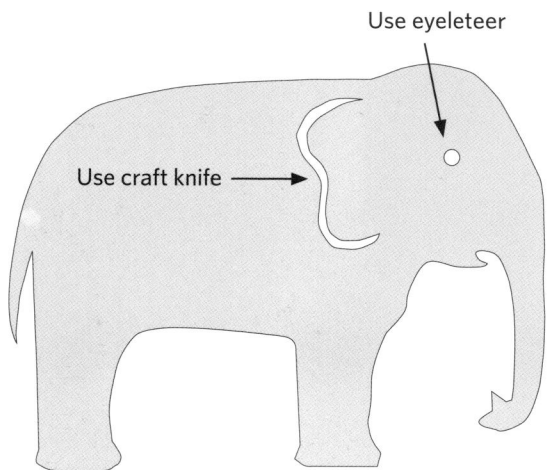

Use eyeleteer

Use craft knife

85 HIPPOPOTAMUS

Tools: Scissors, eyeleteer
Folding Technique: No fold

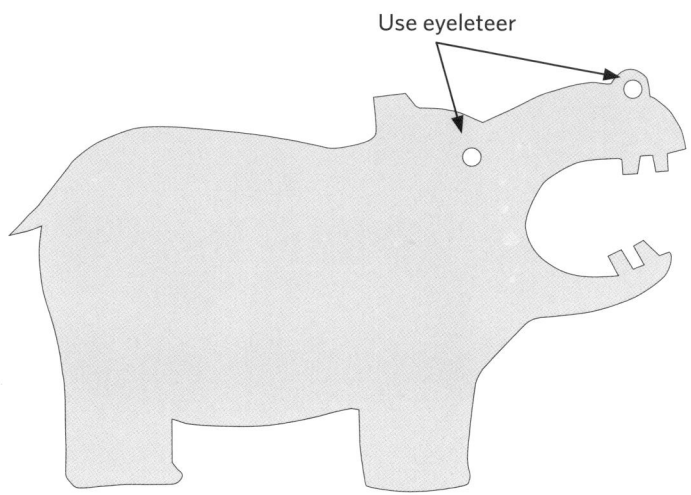

Use eyeleteer

86 ZEBRA

Tools: Scissors, craft knife
Folding Technique: No fold

Use scissors for the outline and
a craft knife for all other cuts

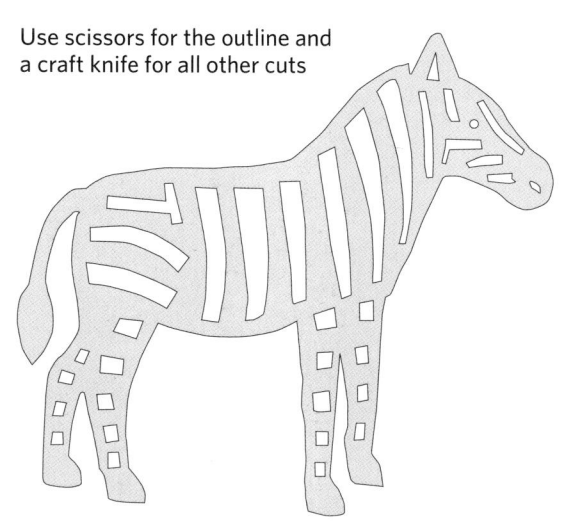

90 SWAN

Tools: Scissors, craft knife
Folding Technique: No fold

Use craft knife or
eyeleteer to cut
out the eye

Use craft knife

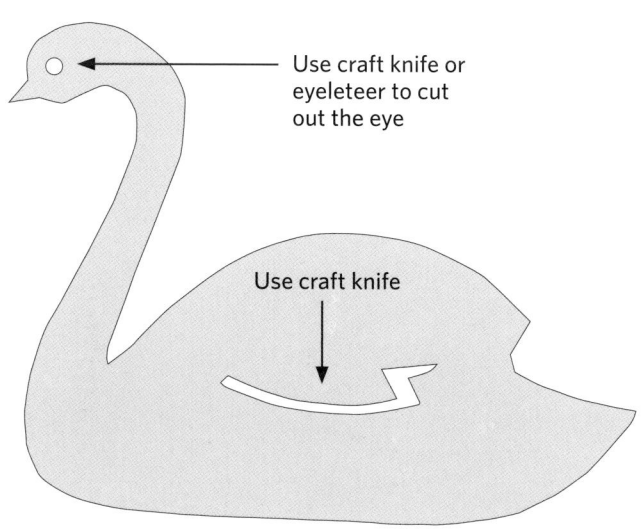

87 GRASS

Tools: Scissors
Folding Technique: Double accordion fold

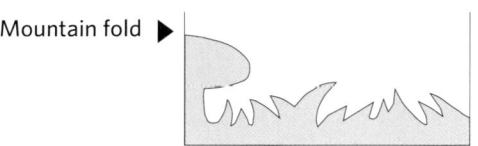

Mountain fold ▶

88 IGLOO

Tools: Scissors, craft knife
Folding Technique: Single geometric fold

Mountain ▶
fold

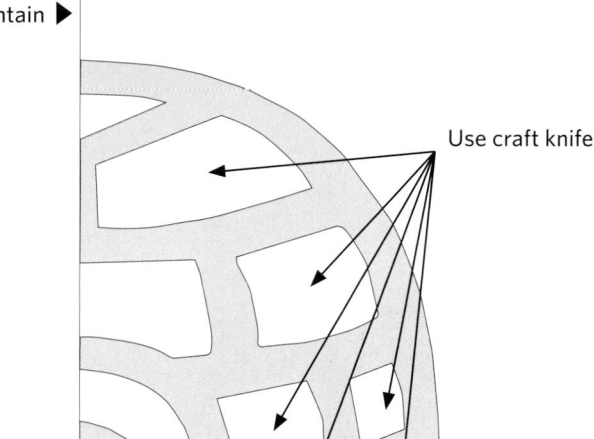

Use craft knife

91 FLAMINGOS

Tools: Scissors, craft knife
Folding Technique: Quadruple geometric fold

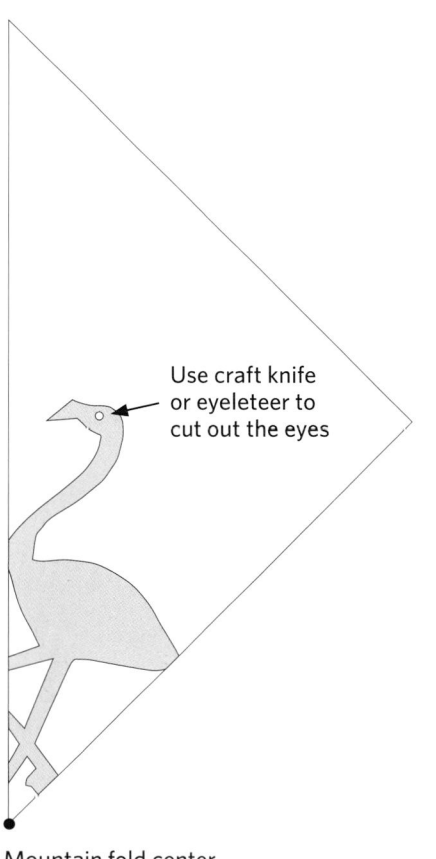

Use craft knife
or eyeleteer to
cut out the eyes

Mountain fold center

89 PENGUINS

Tools: Scissors, craft knife, eyeleteer
Folding Technique: Double accordion fold

Mountain fold ▶   Use eyeleteer

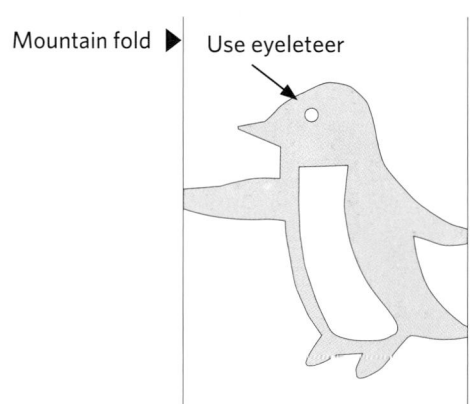

HOLIDAYS

92 Gift | **93** Circle of Hearts | **94** Heart Motif |
95 Chocolate | *Templates on pages 80–81*

93

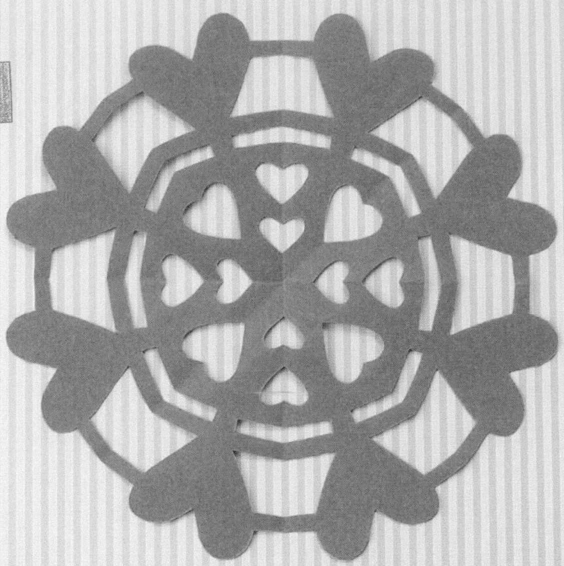

92

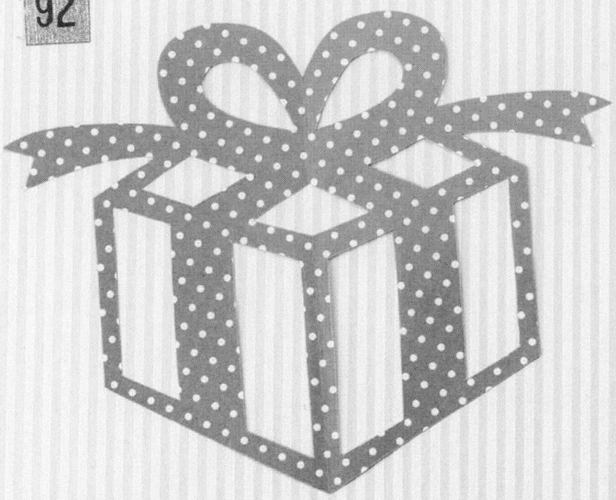

94

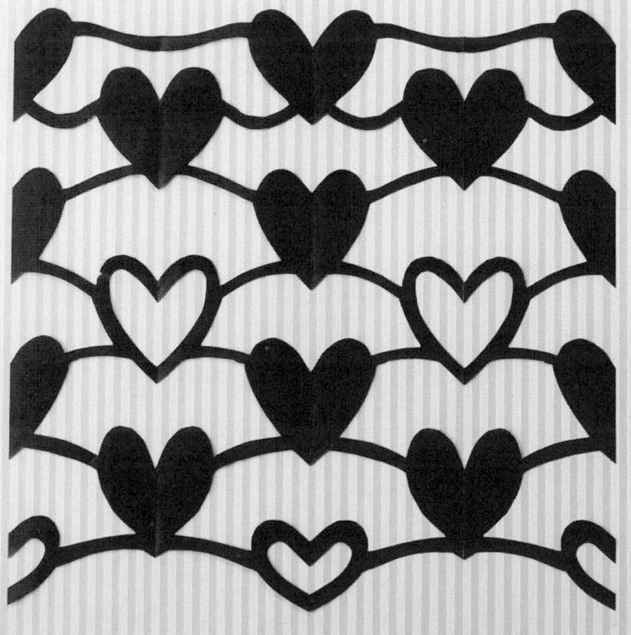

95

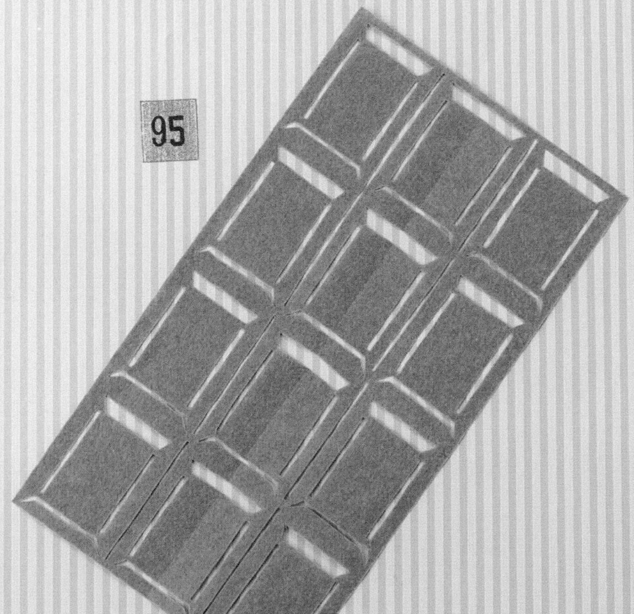

97

98

96

100

99

101

92 GIFT

Tools: Scissors, craft knife
Folding Technique: Single geometric fold

Mountain ▶
fold

Use craft knife

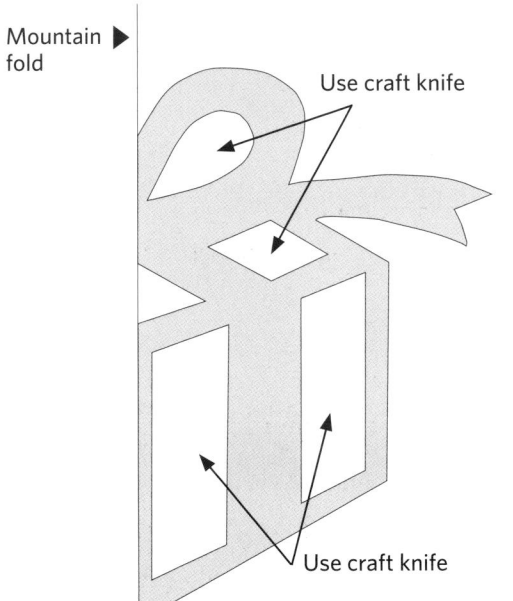

Use craft knife

93 CIRCLE OF HEARTS

Tools: Scissors
Folding Technique: Quadruple geometric fold

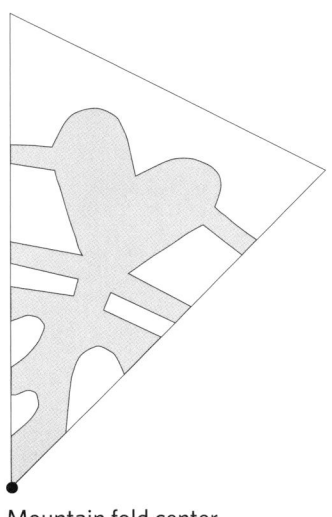

Mountain fold center

Decorate the lid of a gift box with one of these Valentine's Day inspired motifs. The Circle of Hearts motif makes a sweet addition to a box of chocolate.

94 HEART MOTIF

Tools: Scissors
Folding Technique: Double accordion fold

Mountain fold ▶

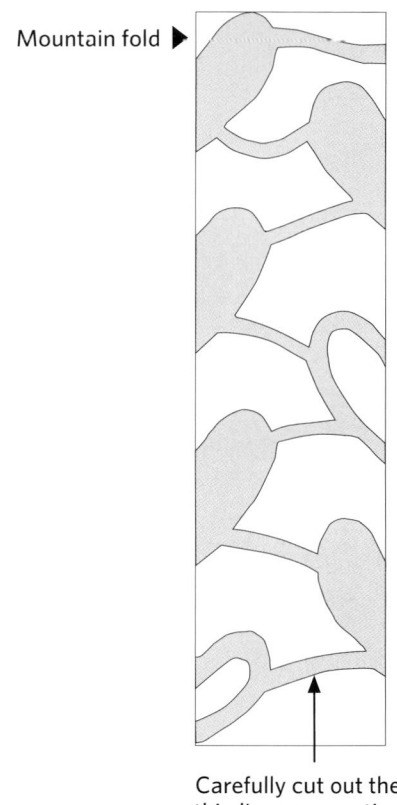

Carefully cut out the
thin lines connecting
the hearts

95 CHOCOLATE

Tools: Scissors, craft knife
Folding Technique: Single geometric fold

Mountain fold ▶

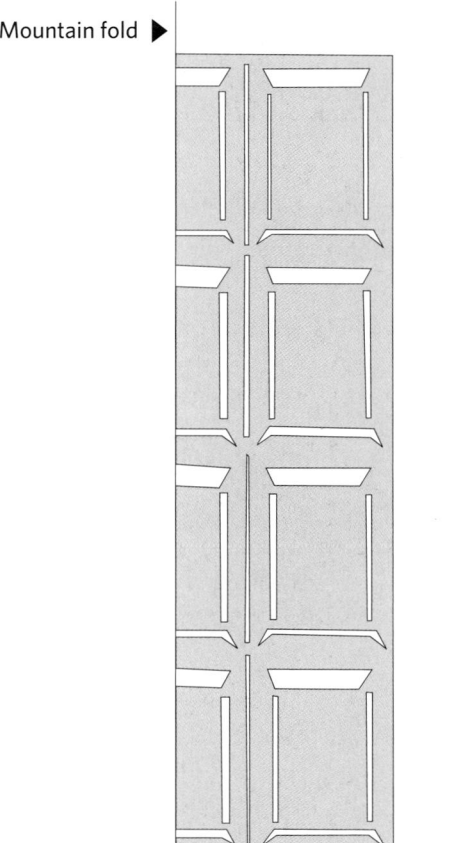

Use scissors for the outline and
a craft knife for all other cuts

96 GHOSTS

Tools: Scissors, craft knife
Folding Technique: Single geometric fold

Use craft knife

Mountain fold ▶

97 WITCH HAT

Tools: Scissors, craft knife
Folding Technique: No fold

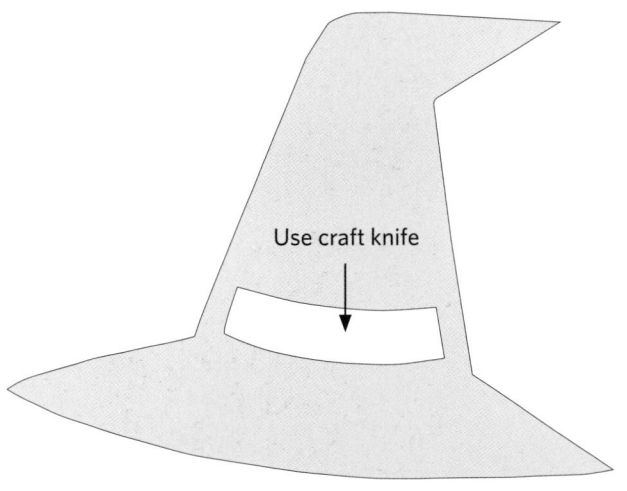

Use craft knife

98 BAT

Tools: Scissors
Folding Technique: Single geometric fold

Mountain fold ▶

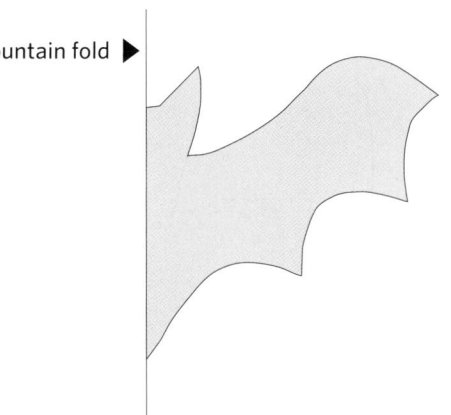

99 CANDY

Tools: Scissors
Folding Technique: Sextuple geometric fold

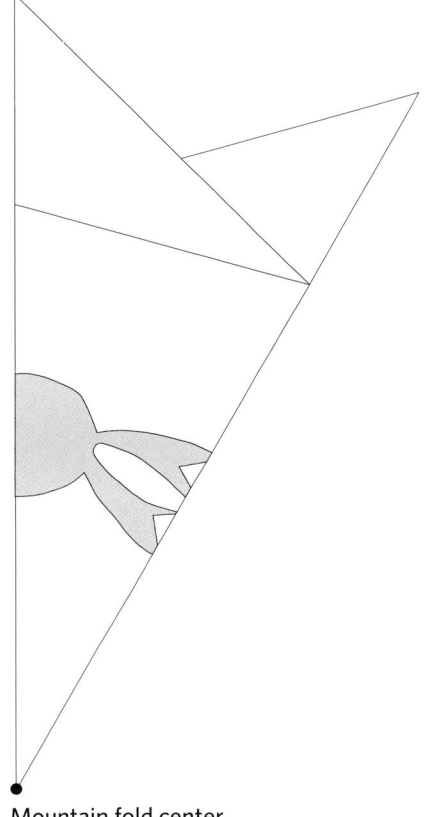

Mountain fold center

100 JACK-O'-LANTERN

Tools: Scissors, craft knife
Folding Technique: Single geometric fold

Mountain fold ▶

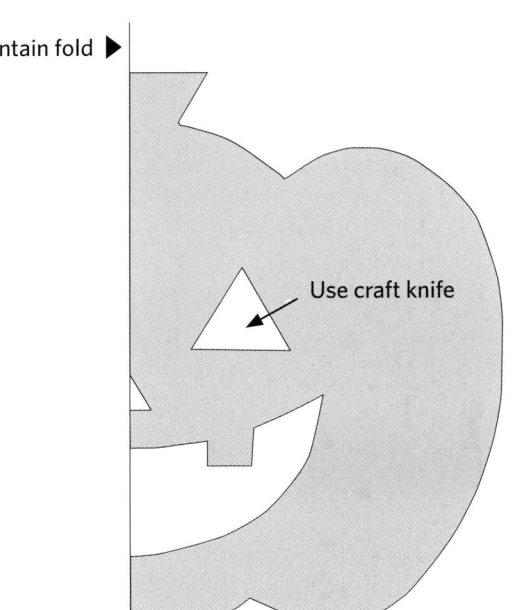

Use craft knife

101 BLACK CAT

Tools: Scissors, craft knife
Folding Technique: No fold

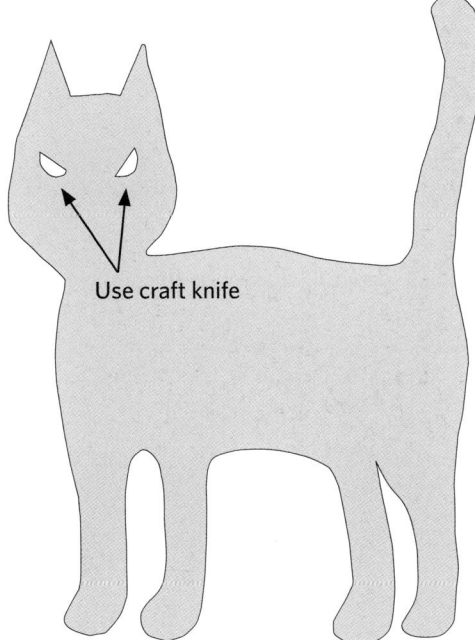

Use craft knife

102 Wreath | **103** Snowflake | **104** Candle |
105 Snowman | *Templates on pages 86–87*

106 Stars | **107** Star Snowflake | **108** Santa |
109 Christmas Tree | *Templates on pages 87–89*

102 WREATH

Tools: Scissors, craft knife
Folding Technique: Single geometric fold

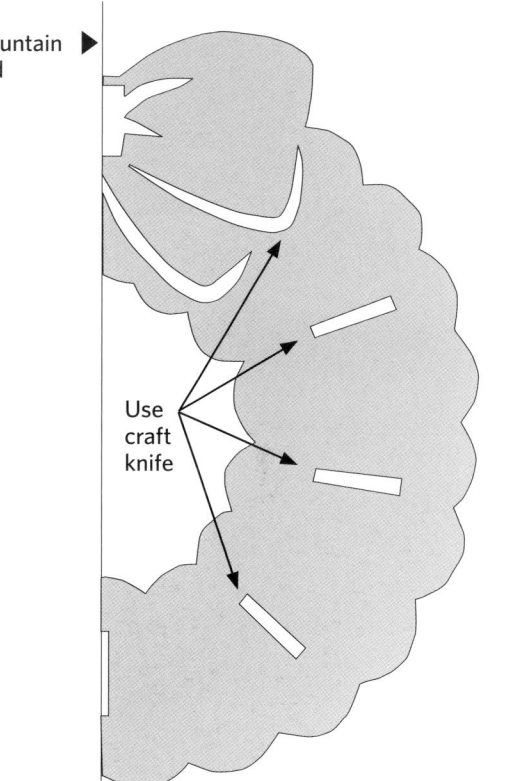

Mountain fold ▶

Use craft knife

103 SNOWFLAKE

Tools: Scissors
Folding Technique: Sextuple geometric fold

Mountain fold center

104 CANDLE

Tools: Scissors, craft knife
Folding Technique: Single geometric fold

Mountain ▶
fold

Use craft
knife

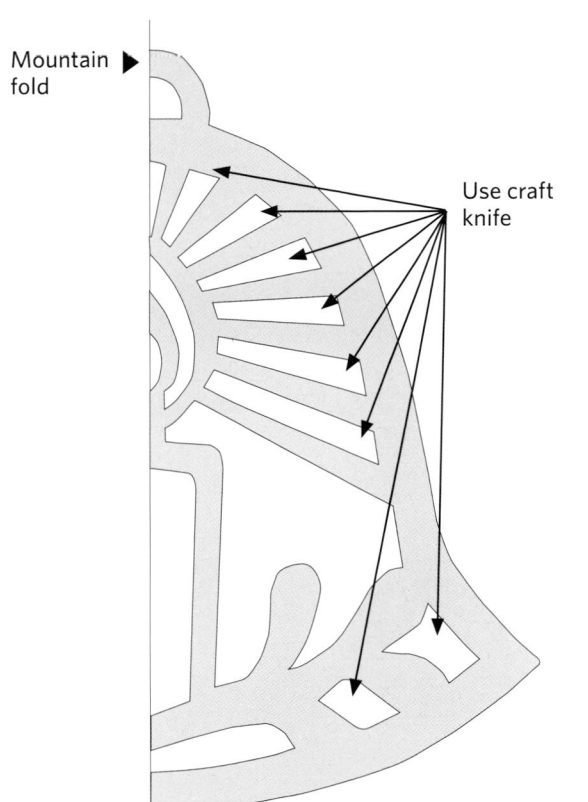

105 SNOWMAN

Tools: Scissors, craft knife
Folding Technique: Single geometric fold

Mountain ▶
fold

Use craft knife

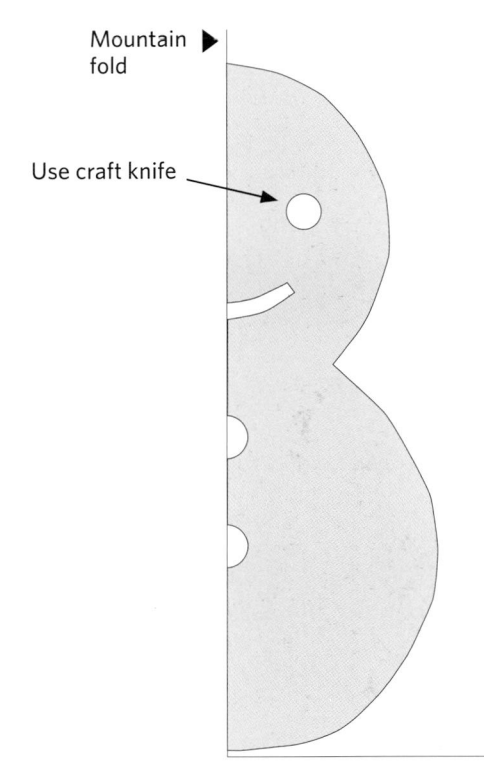

106 STARS

Tools: Scissors

Folding Technique: Triple accordion fold

Note: For the variation with four stars (refer to page 85), use the quadruple accordion fold.

Mountain ▶
fold

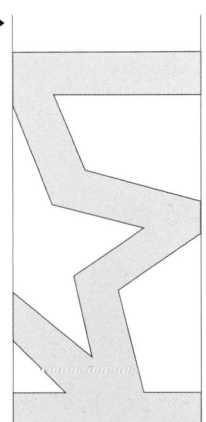

107 STAR SNOWFLAKE

Tools: Scissors

Folding Technique: Sextuple geometric fold

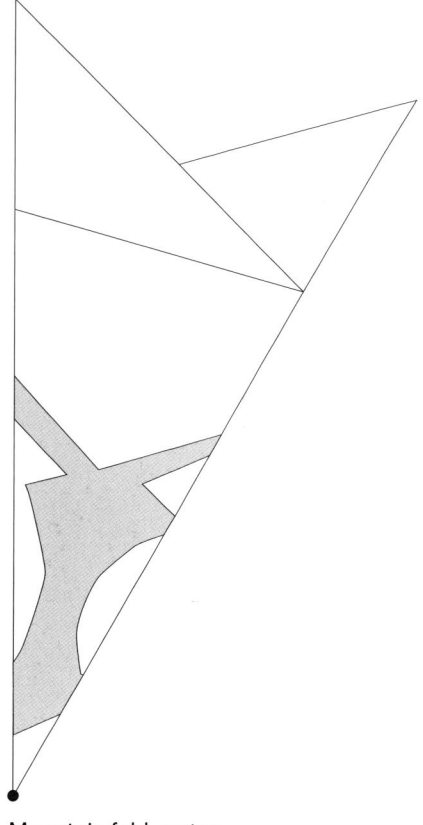

Mountain fold center

109 CHRISTMAS TREE

Tools: Scissors

Folding Technique: Single geometric fold

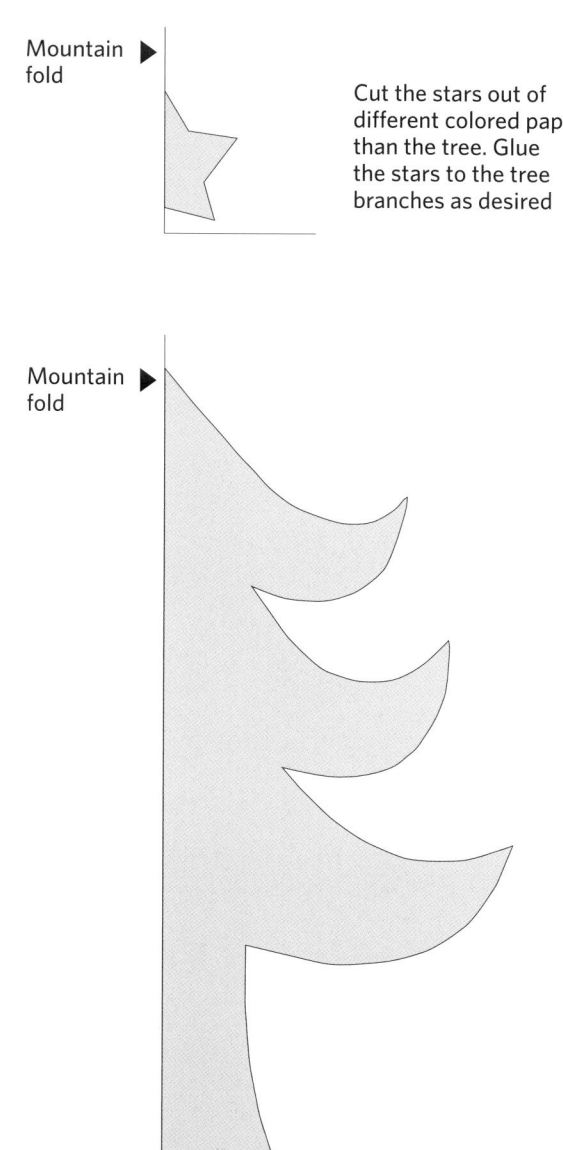

Mountain fold ▶

Cut the stars out of different colored paper than the tree. Glue the stars to the tree branches as desired

Mountain fold ▶

108 SANTA

Tools: Scissors, craft knife

Folding Technique: Single geometric fold

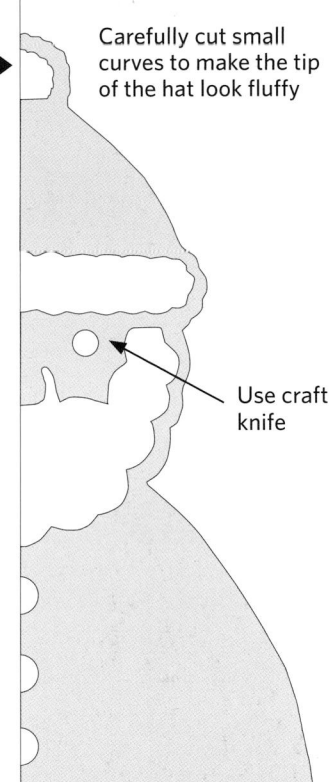

Mountain fold ▶

Carefully cut small curves to make the tip of the hat look fluffy

Use craft knife

Make your own holiday cards by gluing these cheerful motifs to the front of a blank greeting card.

GLOBETROTTING

110

111

112

113

114

110 Airplane | 111 Boat | 112 Car | 113 Tram |
114 Train | *Templates on pages 92–93*

110 AIRPLANE

Tools: Scissors
Folding Technique: Single geometric fold

Mountain fold

112 CAR

Tools: Scissors, craft knife
Folding Technique: Single geometric fold

111 BOAT

Tools: Scissors, craft knife
Folding Technique: No fold

Mountain fold ▶

Use scissors for the outline and a craft knife for all other cuts

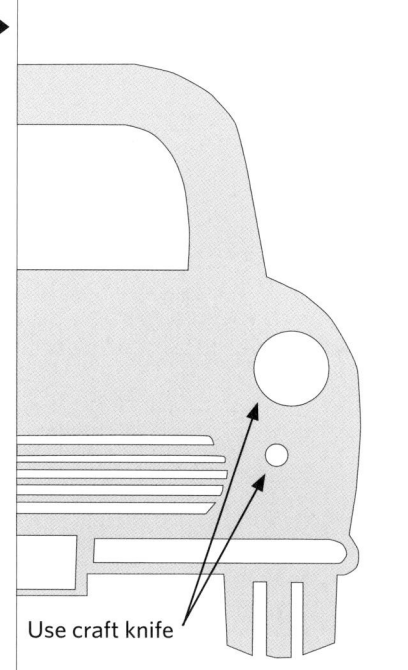

Use craft knife

113 TRAM

Tools: Scissors, craft knife
Folding Technique: Single geometric fold

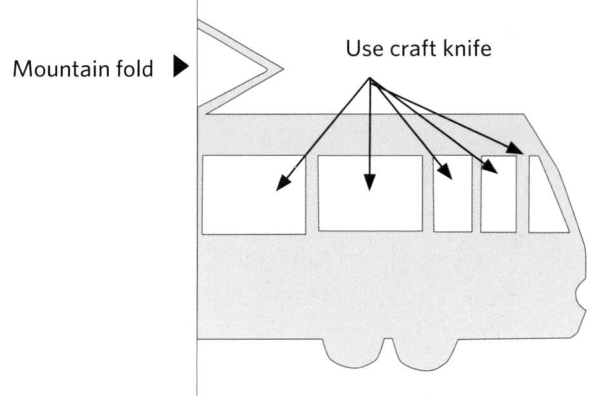

Mountain fold ▶

Use craft knife

114 TRAIN

Tools: Scissors, craft knife
Folding Technique:
A: No fold
B: Single geometric fold

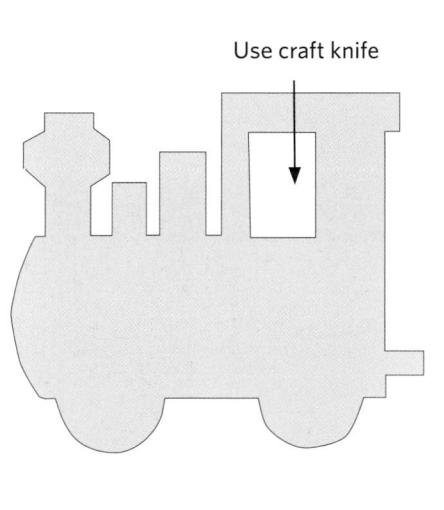

Use craft knife

A

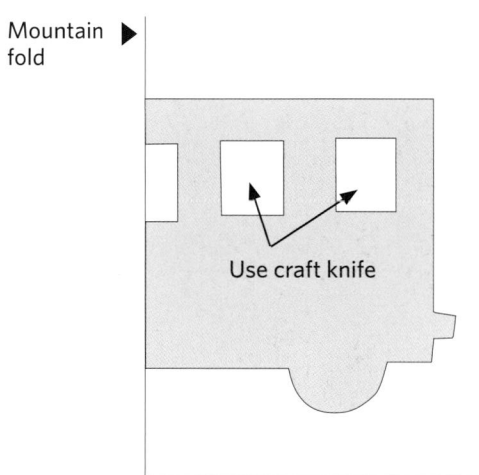

Mountain fold ▶

Use craft knife

B

115

116

118

117

115 Suitcase | 116 Clock | 117 Photo Frame | 118 Camera | 119 Letter | 120 Post Office Symbol | 121 Pen | 122 Post Box |
Templates on pages 96–99

119

120

121

122

115 SUITCASE

Tools: Scissors, craft knife
Folding Technique: Single geometric fold

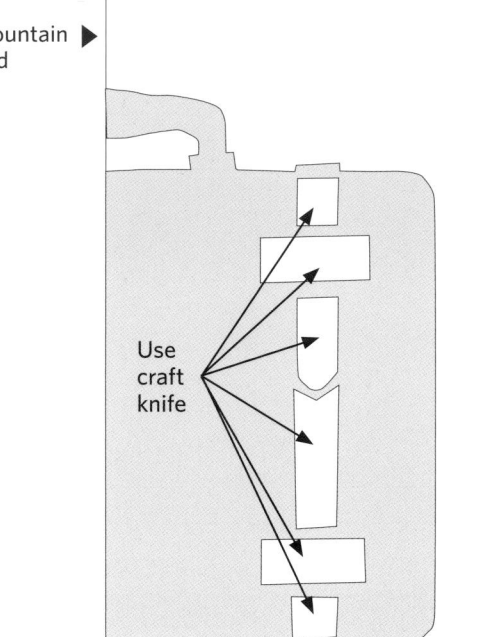

Mountain fold ▶

Use craft knife

116 CLOCK

Tools: Scissors
Folding Technique: Single geometric fold

Mountain fold ▶

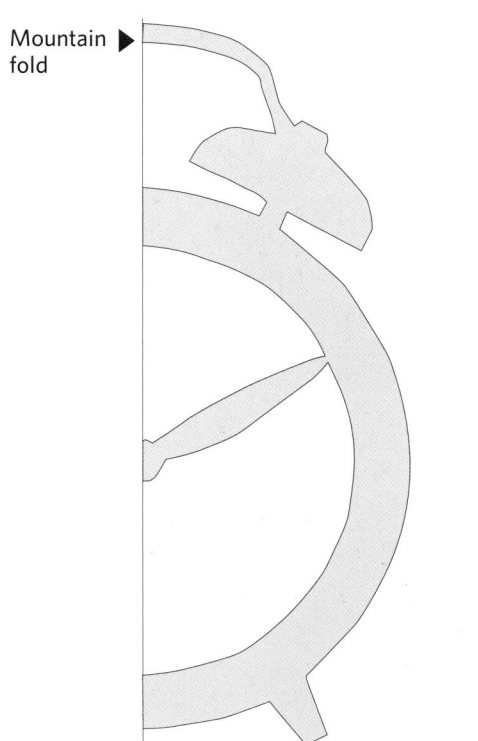

117 PHOTO FRAME

Tools: Scissors

Folding Technique: Double geometric fold

Mountain fold center

Create a special frame to showcase your favorite vacation memories. Embellish a store-bought frame with travel motifs, such as the Photo Frame and Airplane.

118 CAMERA

Tools: Scissors, craft knife
Folding Technique: Single geometric fold

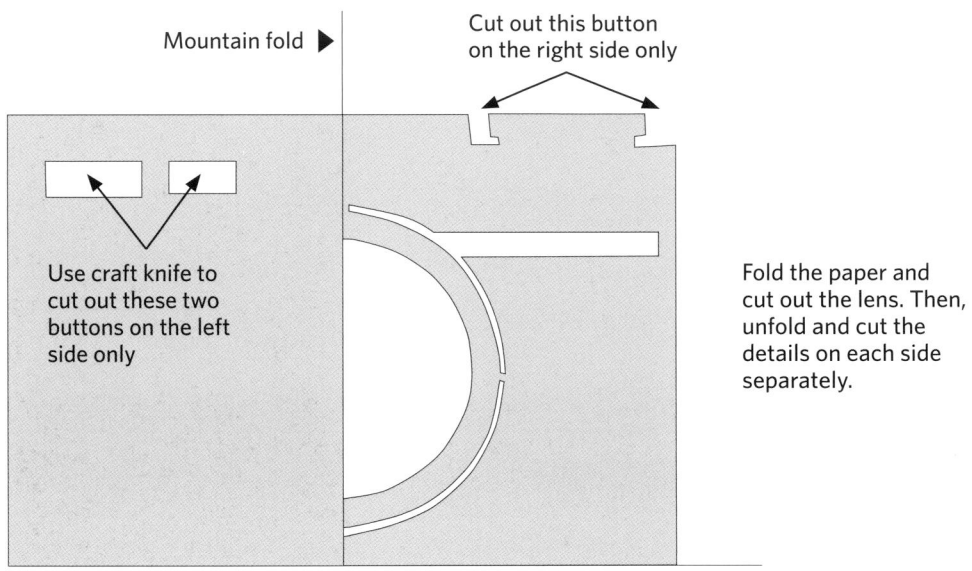

Mountain fold ▶

Cut out this button on the right side only

Use craft knife to cut out these two buttons on the left side only

Fold the paper and cut out the lens. Then, unfold and cut the details on each side separately.

119 LETTER

Tools: Scissors
Folding Technique: Single geometric fold

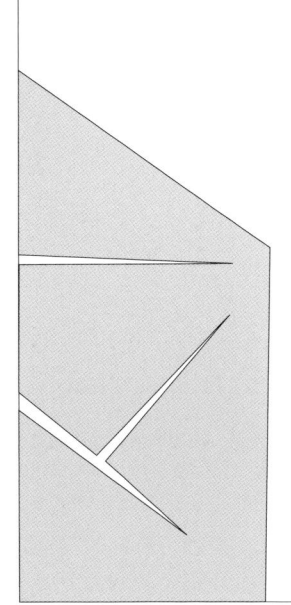

Mountain fold ▶

120 POST OFFICE SYMBOL

Tools: Scissors, craft knife
Folding Technique:
A: No fold
B: Single geometric fold

A

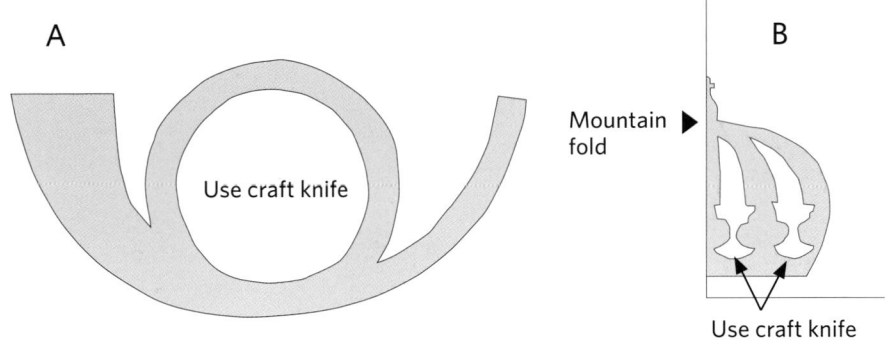

Use craft knife

B

Mountain fold ▶

Use craft knife

121 PEN

Tools: Scissors
Folding Technique: Single geometric fold

Mountain fold ▶

122 POST BOX

Tools: Scissors
Folding Technique: Single geometric fold

Mountain fold ▶

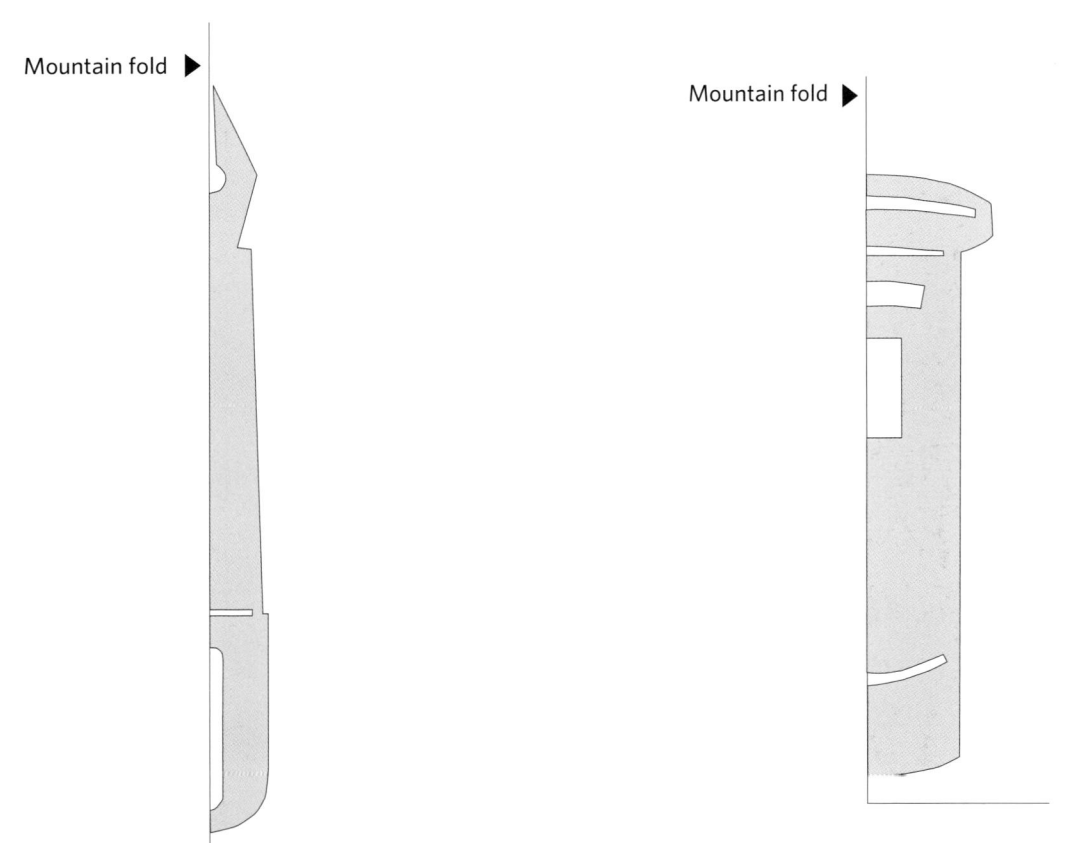

123

124

125

123 Hearts | **124** Shamrocks | **125** Globe |
126 Kids Around the World | **127** Angels |
128 Birds | **129** Chain of Children |
Templates on pages 102–103

126

127

128

129

123 HEARTS

Tools: Scissors
Folding Technique: Quadruple geometric fold

Mountain fold center

124 SHAMROCKS

Tools: Scissors
Folding Technique: Triple geometric fold

Mountain fold center

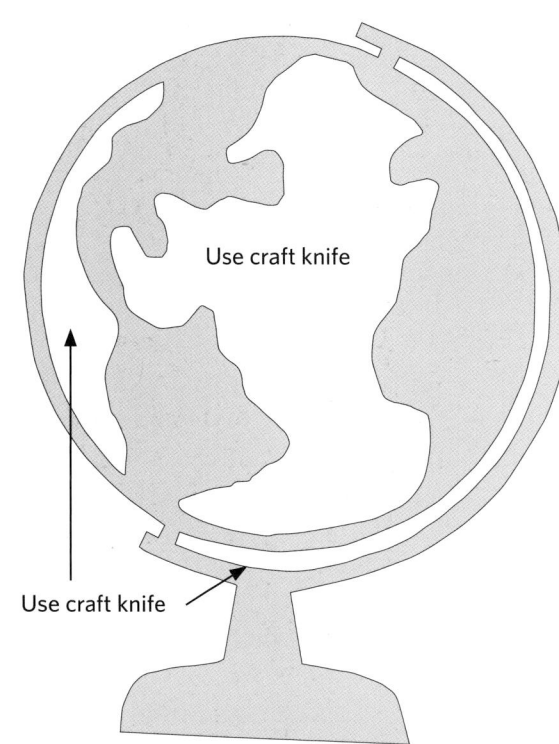

Use craft knife

Use craft knife

125 GLOBE

Tools: Scissors, craft knife
Folding Technique: No fold

126 KIDS AROUND THE WORLD

Tools: Scissors, eyeleteer
Folding Technique: Quadruple geometric fold

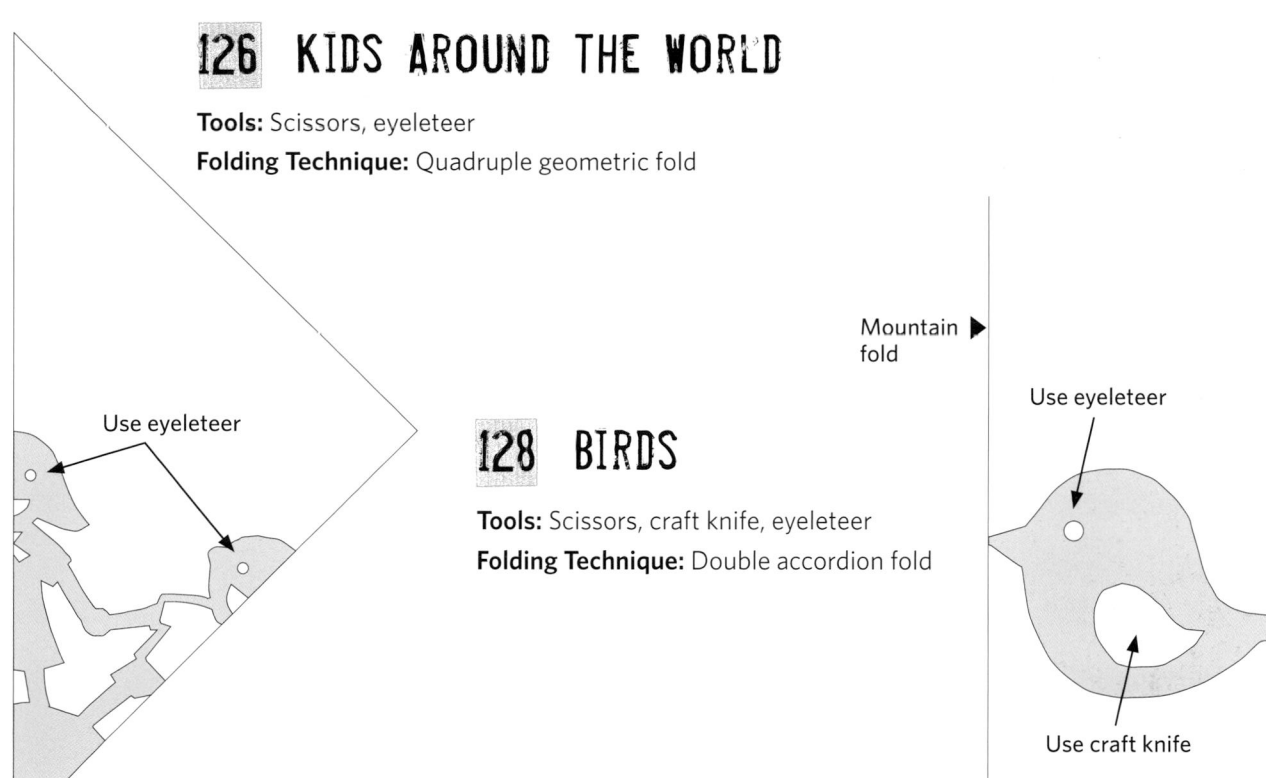

Use eyeleteer

Mountain fold center

128 BIRDS

Tools: Scissors, craft knife, eyeleteer
Folding Technique: Double accordion fold

Mountain fold ▶

Use eyeleteer

Use craft knife

129 CHAIN OF CHILDREN

Tools: Scissors, eyeleteer
Folding Technique:
Triple accordion fold

Mountain fold ▶

Note: To make this project appear as shown on page 101, cut off the extra sections.

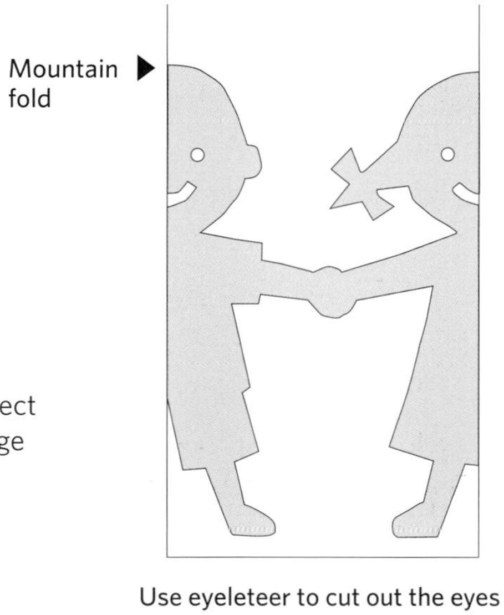

Use eyeleteer to cut out the eyes

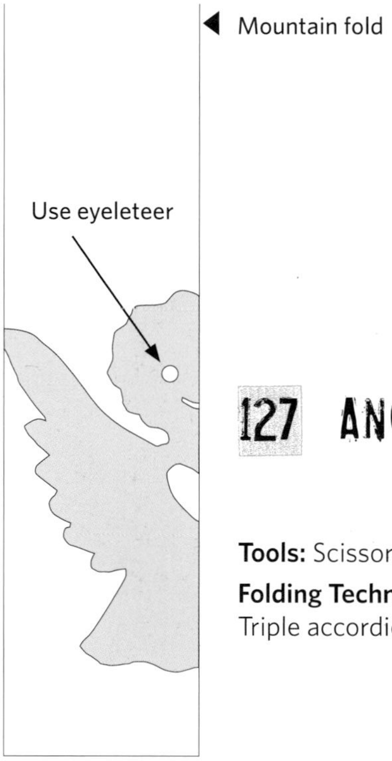

◀ Mountain fold

Use eyeleteer

127 ANGELS

Tools: Scissors, eyeleteer
Folding Technique:
Triple accordion fold

CULTURAL PASTIMES

Motif Collection

130 Teddy Bear | **131** Ballet Slippers | **132** Wooden Toy Horses |
133 Matryoshkas | *Templates on pages 106–107*

130

131

132

133

134

135

136

137

130 TEDDY BEAR

Tools: Scissors, craft knife
Folding Technique: Single geometric fold

Mountain fold ▶

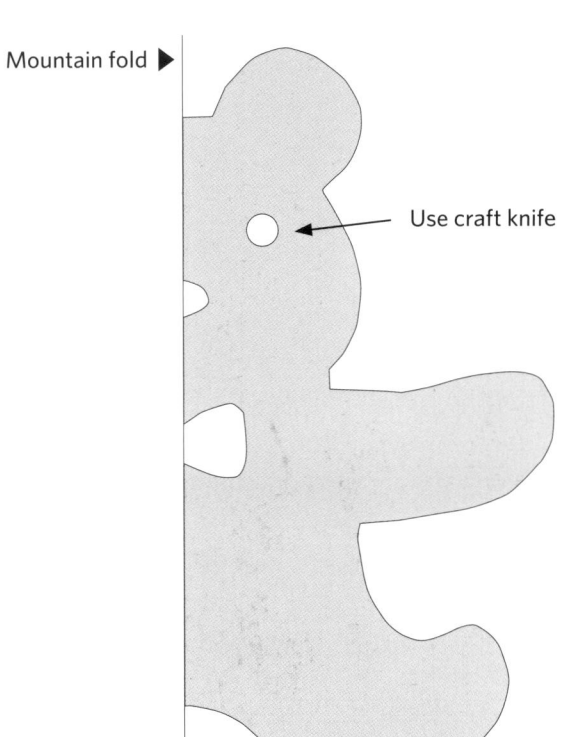

Use craft knife

131 BALLET SLIPPERS

Tools: Scissors, craft knife
Folding Technique: Single geometric fold

Mountain fold ▶

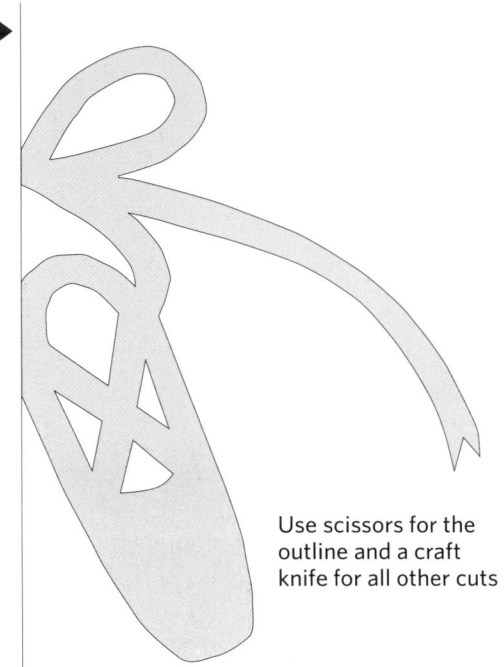

Use scissors for the outline and a craft knife for all other cuts

Create one-of-a-kind bags for all occasions. Decorate your tote bags with motifs that correspond to their use—glue the Ballet Slippers to a child's ballet class bag or the Palette to a bag for art supplies. These motifs are also great for creating gift wrap for presents. Add a Teddy Bear to a gift bag to provide a hint of what's inside.

132 WOODEN TOY HORSES

Tools: Scissors
Folding Technique: Double accordion fold

Mountain ▶
fold

Note: To make this project appear as shown on page 104, cut off the extra sections.

133 MATRYOSHKAS

Tools: Scissors
Folding Technique: Quadruple accordion fold

Mountain fold ▶

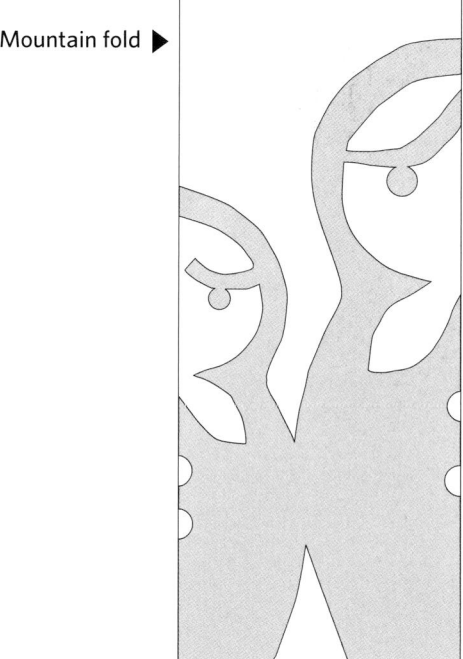

Note: To make this project appear as shown on page 104, cut off the extra sections.

134 EASEL

Tools: Scissors
Folding Technique: Single geometric fold

Mountain fold ▶

135 CRAYON

Tools: Scissors
Folding Technique: Single geometric fold

Mountain fold ▶

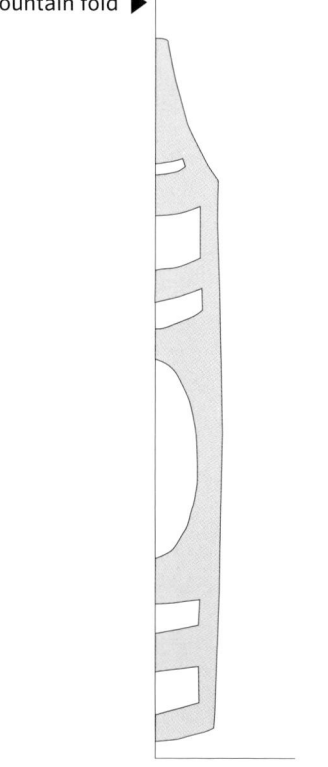

136 PAINT AND BRUSHES

Tools: Scissors, craft knife
Folding Technique: Single geometric fold

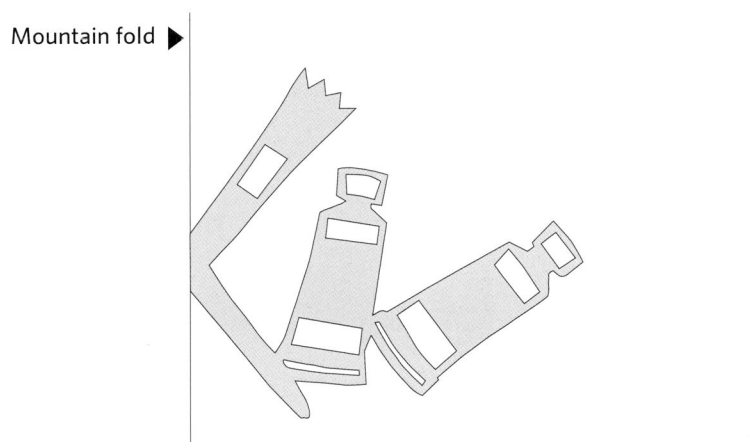

Use scissors for the outline and a craft knife for all other cuts

137 PALETTE

Tools: Scissors, craft knife
Folding Technique: No fold

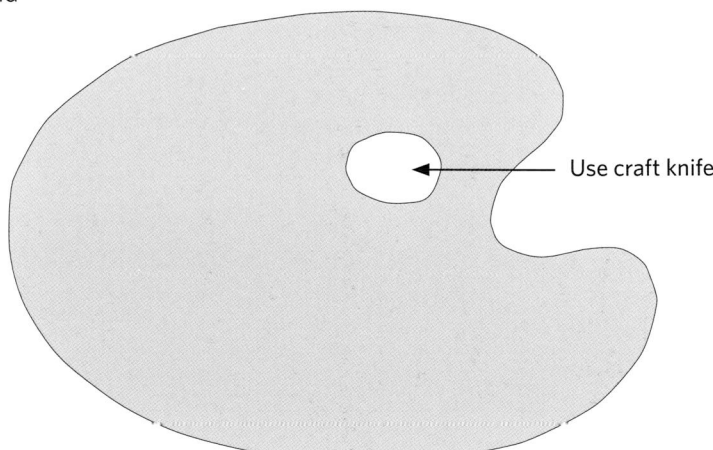

Use craft knife

138 Ribbon | **139** Key | **140** Scalloped Lace | **141** Antique Lace | *Templates on pages 112–113*

142 Scissors | **143** Thread | **144** Sewing Machine |
Templates on pages 112–113

138 RIBBON

Tools: Scissors, craft knife
Folding Technique: Single geometric fold

Mountain ▶
fold

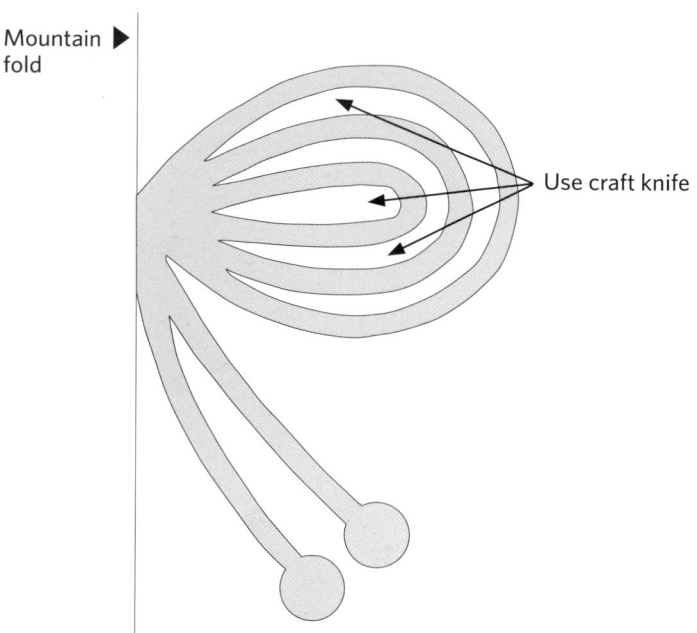

Use craft knife

139 KEY

Tools: Scissors
Folding Technique: Single geometric fold

Mountain ▶
fold

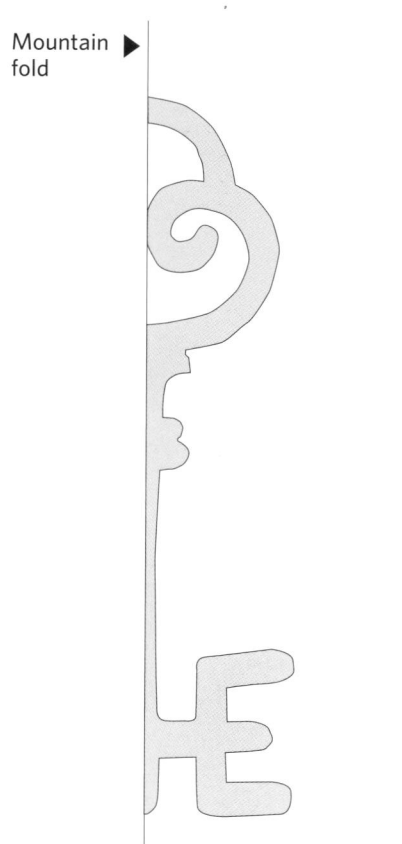

Unfold and cut the teeth out
on one side only

Mountain ▶
fold

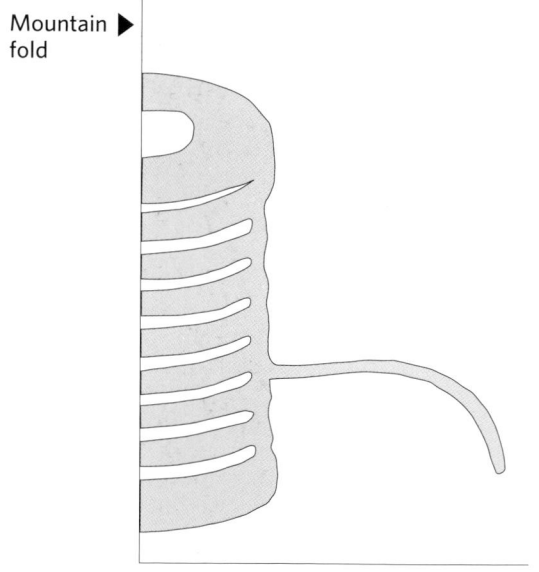

Unfold and cut the strand of thread
out on one side only

143 THREAD

Tools: Scissors
Folding Technique: Single geometric fold

140 SCALLOPED LACE

Tools: Scissors, craft knife
Folding Technique: Quadruple accordion fold

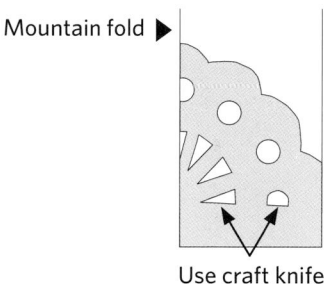

Mountain fold ▶

Use craft knife

141 ANTIQUE LACE

Tools: Scissors, craft knife
Folding Technique: Quadruple accordion fold

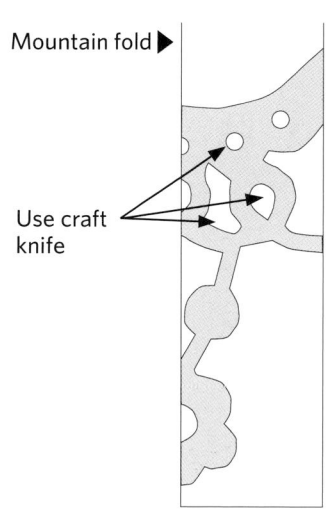

Mountain fold ▶

Use craft knife

These lace motifs serve as the perfect embellishment for trimming greeting cards, notes and invitations.

144 SEWING MACHINE

Tools: Scissors, craft knife
Folding Technique: No fold

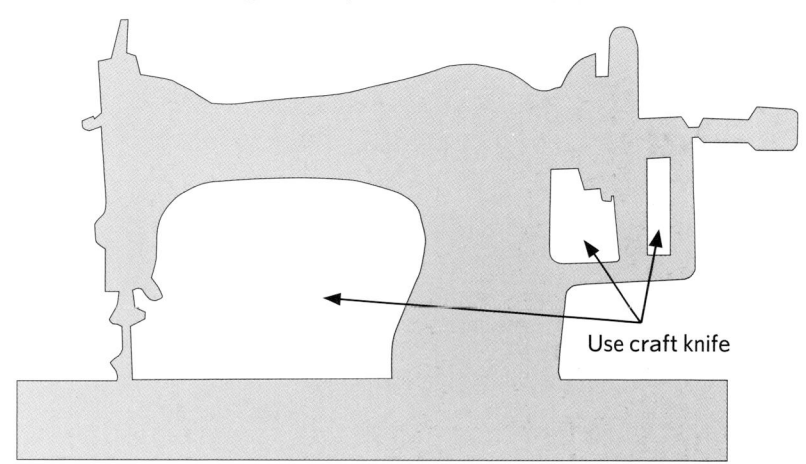

Use craft knife

142 SCISSORS

Tools: Scissors, craft knife
Folding Technique: Sextuple geometric fold

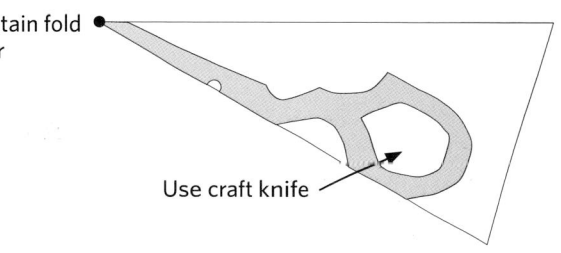

Mountain fold center

Use craft knife

145 Music Note 1 | **146** Choir Boy | **147** Treble Clef |
148 Keyboard | **149** Music Note 2 | **150** Violin |
Templates on pages 116–117

151 | 152 | 153 | 154

151 Marionette | **152** Accordion | **153** Bohemian Glass |
154 Streetlamps | *Templates on pages 118–119*

145 MUSIC NOTE 1

Tools: Scissors
Folding Technique: No fold

147 TREBLE CLEF

Tools: Scissors, craft knife
Folding Technique: No fold

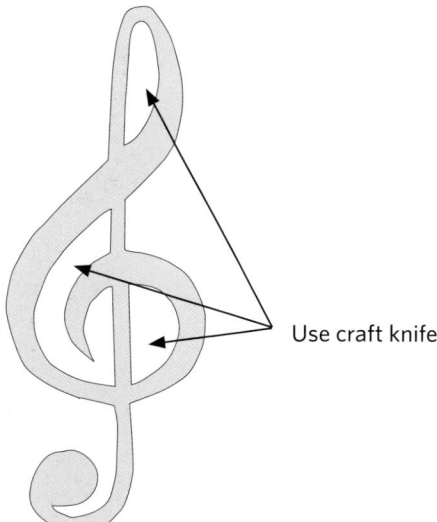

Use craft knife

146 CHOIR BOY

Tools: Scissors, craft knife
Folding Technique: Single geometric fold

Mountain fold ▶

Use craft knife

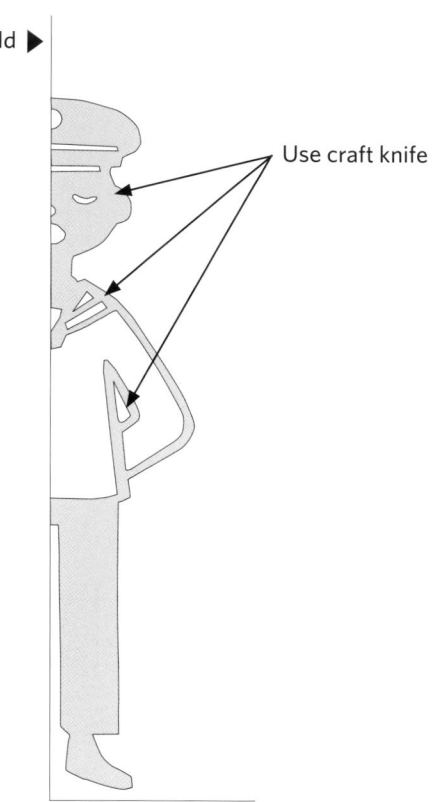

149 MUSIC NOTE 2

Tools: Scissors
Folding Technique: No fold

148 KEYBOARD

Tools: Scissors, craft knife
Folding Technique: Single geometric fold

Mountain fold ▶

Use craft knife to cut out white keys

Note: If you want to create a longer keyboard, use a long piece of paper and the double accordion fold.

150 VIOLIN

Tools: Scissors, craft knife
Folding Technique: Single geometric fold

Mountain fold ▶

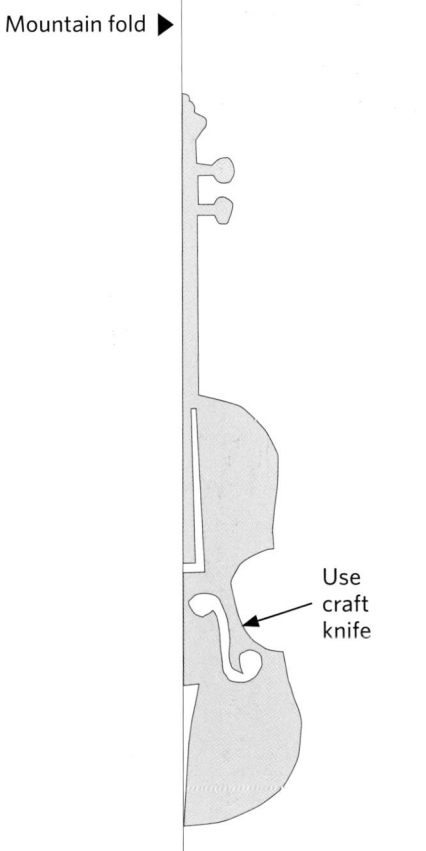

Use craft knife

151 MARIONETTE

Tools: Scissors, craft knife
Folding Technique: Single geometric fold

Mountain fold ▶

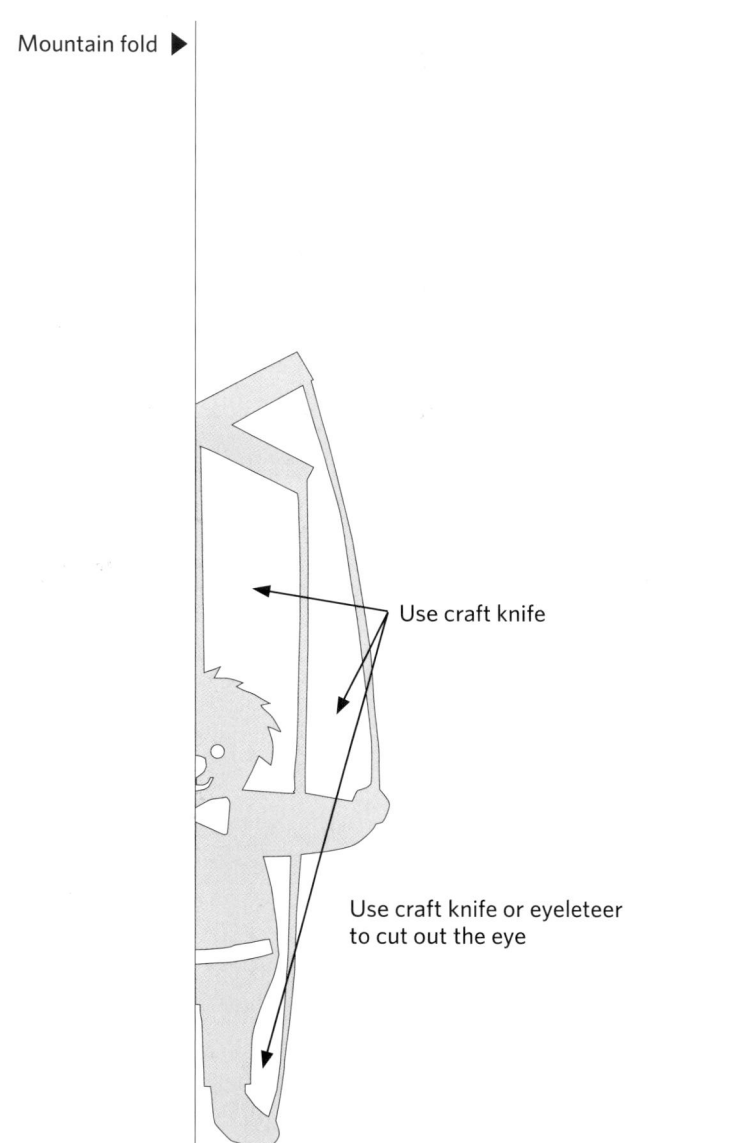

Use craft knife

Use craft knife or eyeleteer
to cut out the eye

152 ACCORDION

Tools: Scissors, craft knife
Folding Technique: No fold

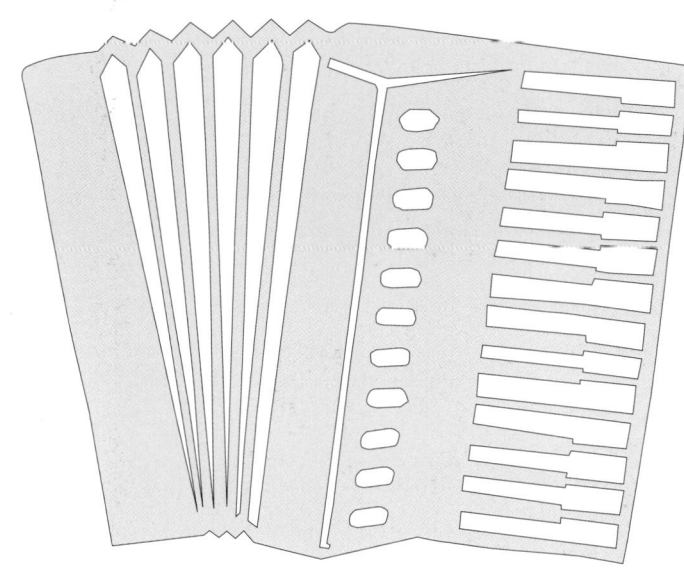

Use scissors for the outline and a craft knife for all other cuts

153 BOHEMIAN GLASS

Tools: Scissors
Folding Technique: Sextuple geometric fold

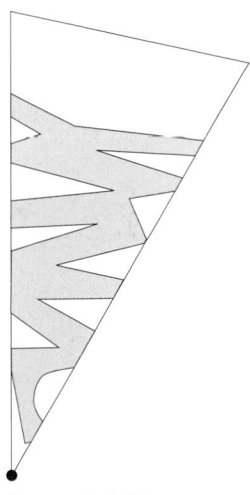

Mountain fold center

154 STREETLAMPS

Tools: Scissors
Folding Technique: Sextuple geometric fold

Mountain fold center

A DAVID & CHARLES BOOK
Copyright ©2012 Boutique-Sha, Inc.

The information in this book was originally published in the following title:
Lady Boutique Series No. 3448 Kirigami de Tanoshimu Sekai no Motif
Copyright ©2012 Boutique-Sha, Inc.
Originally published in Japanese language by Boutique-Sha, Tokyo, Japan
All rights reserved. No part of this book may be reproduced in any form without written
permission from the original proprietor.

Japanese Language Edition Staff:
Editors: Yoko Koike and Yoshiaki Fukuda
Photography: Mari Harada
Layout: Kazue Shibagaki
Illustrations: Kyoko Nagahama and Ogiwara Kikaku

English language translation & production by World Book Media, LLC.
Email: info@worldbookmedia.com
English Translation: Asako Ohashi
English Language Editor: Lindsay Fair

First published in the UK and USA in 2013 by F&W Media International, LTD.
David & Charles is an imprint of F&W Media International, LTD.
Brunel House, Forde Close, Newton Abbot, TQ12 4PU, UK

F&W Media International, Ltd is a subsidiary of F+W Media, Inc.
10151 Carver Road, Suite #200, Blue Ash, OH 45242, USA

ISBN-13: 978-1-4463-0351-1 paperback
ISBN-10: 1-4463-0351-9 paperback

Printed in China
10 9 8 7 6 5 4 3 2 1

F+W Media publishes high quality books on a wide range of subjects.
For more great book ideas visit: www.stitchcraftcreate.co.uk